STAND UP AND BE COUNTED

Stand Up and Be Counted provides middle leaders with increased knowledge, understanding and confidence in the leadership process. It examines the qualities that enable middle leaders to lead effectively and have a positive impact on the vision and culture of their school.

With clear explanations of leadership theory, chapters cover a wide range of topics such as recruitment, coaching staff, crisis management, teamwork, setting standards, dealing with inspections, and evaluating both your own and staff performance. Full of real examples of leadership situations in schools and opportunities to reflect, this book will help middle leaders to develop the habits and skills they need to be successful in their roles. This inspirational and conceptual book:

- acknowledges the essentials of leadership and decision-making;
- highlights how teachers become leaders, including the initial status of followership;
- discusses the good habits and skills that teachers can adopt to prepare themselves for leadership roles;
- identifies key concepts for middle leaders such as vision, inspiration, courage, and self-belief;
- addresses the need to be a visionary and lead from the front: to be courageous.

Covering all aspects of leadership and using examples from various walks of life to illuminate the role of a leader, this book will be of great interest to middle leaders across the primary and secondary sectors as well as subject leaders looking to increase their knowledge and confidence in their development.

Trevor Kerry has been a teacher in primary, secondary, and further education. He worked for several innovative government-funded projects, as well as being a teacher educator, LEA senior adviser, and academic. He has written more than 30 education texts and is Emeritus Professor of Educational Leadership in the University of Lincoln, UK, and Visiting Professor at Bishop Grosseteste University, Lincoln.

'This book is a must have for every aspiring leader in education! Through his vast knowledge and experience in the field of Educational Leadership and Management Prof. Kerry suggests ways to hone and improve on skills to do the job in a more thoughtful and reflective way'.

M. Bondin, Head of school, St Benedict College, Malta

'Trevor's authority in leadership development shines through the style, and diversity of anecdotal evidence and narratives. The parallels between military education, and other sectors, have not been highlighted as overtly in the literature as in this volume. The book is a great addition for refreshing policies and programmes in leadership development'.

Dr Terfot A. Ngwana, Leadership Academic, University of Wales Trinity Saint David, London, UK

STAND UP AND
BE COUNTED

MIDDLE LEADERSHIP IN
EDUCATION CONTEXTS

Trevor Kerry

Routledge
Taylor & Francis Group

LONDON AND NEW YORK

First published 2021
by Routledge
2 Park Square, Milton Park, Abingdon, Oxon OX14 4RN

and by Routledge
52 Vanderbilt Avenue, New York, NY 10017

Routledge is an imprint of the Taylor & Francis Group, an informa business

British Library Cataloguing-in-Publication Data
A catalogue record for this book is available from the British Library

Library of Congress Cataloging-in-Publication Data
Names: Kerry, Trevor, author.
Title: Stand up and be counted : middle leadership in education contexts / Trevor Kerry.
Description: Abingdon, Oxon ; New York, NY : Routledge, 2021. | Includes bibliographical references and index. |
Identifiers: LCCN 2020038766 | ISBN 9780367553159 (hardback) | ISBN 9780367553142 (paperback) | ISBN 9781003092957 (ebook)
Subjects: LCSH: School management and organization. | Middle managers.
Classification: LCC LB2805 .K395 2021 | DDC 371.2/011–dc23
LC record available at https://lccn.loc.gov/2020038766

ISBN: 978-0-367-55315-9 (hbk)
ISBN: 978-0-367-55314-2 (pbk)
ISBN: 978-1-003-09295-7 (ebk)

Typeset in Bembo
by Newgen Publishing UK

You are on a journey...

It is a leadership journey. It is not without risk.

On the way you will gain new knowledge, adopt new ways of looking at situations, understand people differently, and find new forms of thinking and working.

Those around you may not appreciate how and why you are changing – yet the journey will change you.

Enjoy the journey and remember:

a rolling stone gathers no moss – active people do not stagnate.

CONTENTS

List of tables   ix
About the author   x
About this book   xi

1 Beginning leading: Great leaders select themselves –
   or do they?   1

2 The boot camp of leadership: Nanson maintains that
   a perfectly folded sock can be a path to greatness   14

3 Thinking in a crisis: Panic destroys reasoned thought   27

4 Only the best – adopting a quality standard:
   The swagger stick of leadership   35

5 The leader as a team player: Bonding, valuing, and
   listening to the band   45

6 Setting an example – having a vision and leading from
   the front: Developing the courage to lead   56

7 The importance of planning: The cautionary tale of
   the Typhoon jet   67

8 Mark time, slow time, quick time: Time as a
   leadership ally   78

9   Becoming élite: Developing and furthering your skills:
    Stand still to drop dead: The need to advance your
    leadership skills and career   89

10 Leaders in context: Leadership across institutional
    styles   99

11 Swift and bold: Completing your leadership journey   106

    Notes   110
    Index   113

TABLES

3.1 Pro forma for interrogating your diary or log 33
5.1 Belbin's team roles 52
9.1 Types of research carried out by teachers 97

ABOUT THE AUTHOR

Trevor Kerry has held posts in primary, secondary, and further education, which included subject leader, head of department, SENCO, and head of campus. He also had appointments in teacher education as subject lecturer, head of department, and principal lecturer for research. He spent various periods as researcher or co-ordinator with Government-funded projects in primary and secondary education, as well as four years as a senior adviser for a local authority and then a spell as a staff tutor for the Open University. His 'retirement' was marked by a return to teach half-time in primary classrooms alongside doctoral tuition: at one point his youngest student was aged four and the oldest 92. He has been professor of education with the College of Teachers, professor of education leadership in the International Institute of Education Leadership at Lincoln University, and is currently emeritus professor of education leadership at Lincoln University and visiting professor in education at Bishop Grosseteste University, Lincoln. He has contributed numerous articles to education journals and written or edited 30 education texts; he has been especially closely associated with ongoing activities for Maltese educators and pupils. Along with spells as Chair and governor in two outstanding secondary schools, Trevor enjoyed freelance journalism, writing on politics, social affairs, consumer issues, and wildlife. Beyond this, his interests span advanced driving, WW2 history, eco-history, aspects of theology, and photography, in which last he has gained over 50 awards in international competitions.

ABOUT THIS BOOK

This is a book about leadership in education. It is aimed at middle leaders in schools: at aspiring and beginning leaders, at colleagues in the early stages of their leadership careers, and at those with some experience who want to recharge their batteries. When the text refers simply to 'leaders' it indicates those groups identified above. The text deals mainly with primary and secondary schools but is relevant to people involved with education 16–18 in other contexts, too. Occasionally, the book mentions heads, principals, or senior management teams: this is to alert you to the problems that occur elsewhere in the school or to focus for a moment on your potential future career.

The idea for the book had its genesis in an unusual way. I saw an advertisement to the effect that the Commandant of the Royal Military Academy Sandhurst, Major General Paul Nanson, was about to publish a volume about the distinctive leadership training given to officer cadets there[1]. Having a practical and theoretical background in leadership, I thought it would be a good read and an interesting comparison with the world of education. This it proved to be.

Nanson's book made me want to produce something similar for the teaching profession. Teachers did not start with the same advantages as the Sandhurst cadets: they were chosen for the profession rather than for a leadership role within it, which emerged only later; they did not have the shared experience of a single training institution which could provide the bedrock of their future careers. There was not the same camaraderie and shared intention.

But there were overlaps – surprisingly frequent overlaps – in the approaches to leadership needed by the officer cadets and the teaching profession. Combined with my other interest – in the links, but more often contrasts, between teacher-leaders and business leaders – a writing project seemed feasible. But the reader needs to be clear: this is not a militaristic book; it does not say schools should be run like a military institution, nor does it say schools should adopt military values. What it does do is extract some of the excellent leadership qualities that are taught in the military leadership field, applying their insights to education contexts: many former military personnel gain high civilian leadership posts for good reason. It uses military metaphors (along with other metaphors) to illuminate the leadership process.

My next decision was about the style of the resulting book and (spurred on in part by Nanson's book) I opted out of the academic approach. This book, then, is not an academic text: it does not have a technical prose style, long lists of references, or scholarly theorising. It is a concept book whose intention is to inspire and encourage.

It does have a narrative form, often in the first person, addressed directly to the reader: a text that comes out of experience, real examples (albeit anonymised), and useful metaphors. The examples are based on actual events, but changed slightly, anonymised, the locations altered, and genders also changed – all of this on a random basis. There are a few notes, indicated by superscript numerals, which allow you to follow up ideas which are interesting but not essential to the main text: these are kept to a minimum, since most things can be Googled these days. Key concepts are flagged up in the chapter heads. The text is broken up (using asterisks) into quite short episodes. The intention is for the reader to dip in and out of the book, not necessarily to read it sequentially or in one sitting. It is a book to put in your pocket for a gruelling trip on public transport or to keep by the bed for episodes of insomnia. It is, in short, a kind of *vade mecum*. It is about doing the job in a thoughtful and reflective way, not about substituting reflection for action.

Various colleagues showed faith in the project. Annamarie Kino and Anna Clarkson at Routledge signalled an immediate enthusiasm. Three colleagues were instantly positive: Duncan Caruana, a Maltese deputy head; Dr Terfot Ngwana, a leadership academic in teaching and school business management; and John Richardson, a

Lincolnshire head teacher. Dr Carolle Kerry, as always, generously entertained my obsession with writing and provided insights from her considerable experience as a former primary school governor and Chair of Governors. My thanks to them. If you gain from this book you can tell me how @LancasterDV403.

BEGINNING LEADING

Great leaders select
themselves – or do they?

**PROFESSIONALISM FOLLOWERSHIP VISION
INSPIRATION**

Through the soft light of London's early morning the new, young, unblemished teachers are setting out on their early morning commute to school. It is London's Llareggub, gobbing gulls on the Embankment, as Miss T click-clacks her high-heeled way to the Tube, past rehearsing Guards in their undress uniforms on Whitehall, left-turning, right-wheeling, presenting arms in anticipation of a Royal Birthday. The caterpillar that is Transport for London will snake her through the suburbs to Britehope Academy while she rehearses mentally the French verbs that Year 10 will conjugate wrongly later, and wishes it were to a waiter in a little French bistro with breakfast croissants beside a soft Mediterranean. Roy Minton Rhodes, geographer, drags a weary Welsh foot out of his grey semi in Croydon that should be white, a now pollution-kippered former-rural idyll, leaving his still somnolent partner in bed, and takes the overground that doesn't have the advantage of blocking out the view with tunnels, imagining in his mind's eye an ox-bow lake seen from the air, preferably about a thousand miles south of here. A red double-decker, foetid with last night's alcohol and green ginger curry, struggles through the shopping streets of Peckham which will later be crammed with pedestrians but now play host to sinister crowds of obese pigeons and inky corvids picking over the litter-bins and on past the Rye, that once was actually countryside, carrying Denby to magic mathematics with the Year 7s. Britehope calls them all; and with the new day, aspirations are rising in their respective breasts, contemplating their future careers in the world of education they have begun to inhabit.

★★★

A colleague of mine, Professor Angela Thody, pointed out very aptly that most of us start the leadership journey by being followers. Our awareness of leadership begins by watching it in action.

Cast your mind back to your first day in the teaching profession. Did you have a leadership role back then? Even without one, do you recall feeling tenuous on that first day, in unfamiliar surroundings, doing alien things among people you didn't know? Yet over time, you gained in confidence, and even aspired to be like at least some of the leaders you saw in your workplace.

So how do teachers like you transition from follower to leader? It can happen in many different ways, but the more common routes are:

You start out as a follower (i.e. a team member, a member of staff with no defined responsibility with respect to others), and then your leader, Mrs Z, goes off sick for a few weeks. The head says to you (and maybe to others): 'We have to cover Mrs Z's roles; so you can take on this bit of the leader's work; Miss E can do that bit; and Mr Q can do another portion'. On a temporary basis you have transitioned to being a leader, and you barely noticed the change, perhaps.

Eventually, your sick colleague returns. But the head says to you: 'You did OK with that responsibility I gave you; you can carry on now in that role – it will assist Mrs Z as she gets back into the groove'. So you've made it to being an appointed leader (probably unpaid), albeit on a smallish scale.

Or you might volunteer for a job. You don't lead a subject, a year, or department; but when a school production comes along you become a lynchpin in it. Colleagues notice you have some skill at getting others to do what needs to be done: they see a spark there. They think: those skills are transferable; they ask you to transfer them to a school leadership role on a more permanent basis.

Maybe you work as a follower in a great team and you like the way your leader works. You think, 'I'd like to model myself on him/her'; so you set out to move into a similar role, maybe in a new location.

Some people get frustrated by what they see as poor leadership; they seek out a similar – or even a different – role where they can lead and do it better.

A few people find their follower role comes, right from the begin-ning, with a responsibility to lead some portion of their work.

Others will be what is popularly termed *ambitious*; they know that they want to progress professionally, take on more responsibility, climb the promotion ladder. They like the challenge. They have a thirst for controlling some aspect of their professional work so that they can reflect: 'This is my doing, it works well; I'm proud of that'.

I was interviewing some vocational students once and a candi-date told me he wanted to enter the Church as a profession. I asked him what he wanted to do in the Church. 'Be a bishop', he said. No ambiguity there, then!

Beginning and middle leaders cover a range of roles: subject leaders, heads of department, faculty heads, curriculum co-ordinators, year leaders, pastoral leaders, and so on. (From time to time in this text I may nudge you to look at senior leaders and how they operate; this is an important part of career progression even though it is not the theme of this book.) All of these leadership roles are interesting and important, but none of them escapes the need to work with others (whether as colleagues or in teams), and none is able to escape these interpersonal issues of leadership and followership.

★★★

What I like best about Angela's article[1] is the section where she investigates different types of followership – positive and nega-tive. Without covering the whole ground of her article, it will be interesting to pursue some of the pointers she identifies, though for the present purpose I have adapted, omitted, or re-named some of her categories. In any school team there are likely to be people who fall into these types, and you can try to spot your position in this typ-ology when you yourself are a follower. Followers may act in these types or play these roles either consciously or unconsciously.

Active-passives probably make up the largest number of followers. They support those decisions the leader makes which they favour; they also acquiesce when they are not so enthusi-astic, providing a willing support to the leader without moving beyond passive acceptance.

Exemplaries are probably the next tranche of leaders in waiting: they 'support and work closely with leaders, participate actively in decision making, are willing/able to question and critique leaders' ideas, think independently, are energetic and assertive risk-takers and self-starters'.

Loyalists might be described as the complacent minority, seek a quiet life – they 'logically justify their support for leaders before granting their quietly determined and unwavering loyalty'.

These follower types carry out between them more, or less, essential roles in the team and on behalf of the leader:

• Being handlers of toxicity in the team and beyond it: toxic handlers sense problems arising and cure them before the leaders have to deal with them or even hear about them.
• Being earnest disciples: they absorb and transmit what they have learned from the leader.
• Being sidekicks: these individuals often 'accompany the leader physically but are officially invisible. On this rests their helpfulness; they have little vested interest in the leader's own role but help the leader to make contributions'.

[I had to go back a long way in my own career to envisage when I had a sidekick, but I did. I was in my first year of teaching in a school where over half the staff members had not served more than a year. We had a young man assigned to the staff: I will call him JP. He was a pre-college student, so aged no more than 19. He was to spend a year with us before he went to teacher training. He was paired with me for that dreaded experience – doing Friday duties in the playground of our secondary modern school. The chances of a wet Friday going horribly wrong thanks to a cadre of older, more disaffected, students were considerable. JP did not really have any authority, so I had to take the lead in whatever was necessary. But we developed an intuitive understanding; and JP was my eyes and ears while I dealt with any incidents that arose. You needed eyes in the back of your head because the less amenable students would constantly test young teachers like me. JP was my eyes and ears. We made a good team.]

• Being gatekeepers: they filter 'which of the information/problems/challenges/requests coming to leaders will go to them. They are loyal and organizationally knowledgeable; their value in reducing the burden on the leader is unquestioned'.

- Being muses: that is, people who offer ideas but hand over credit for them to the leader.
- Being aspirants, mentees, apprentices (leadership trainee roles): these are team members who are working towards leadership skills. They may try to impress the leader and will use learning opportunities.
- Being seconds-in-command: 'These followers suppress in public any differences of opinion with the leader, consciously develop skills which the leader does not have or does not choose to have, transmitting them as accurately as possible the leader's views to other followers'.

Inevitably, there are balancing negative types and roles, and we will look at those a bit later in the chapter. At this point I would just flag up the pleasure of working with an *Exemplary*.

It really is a delight to have someone on your team who is in tune with what you are trying to do, and who is aspiring to do something similar in due course. My *Exemplary* was a man about ten years younger than me; but we shared a philosophy about teaching and a view of how leadership should work. This did not prevent him from having his own views in specific situations; and I was always glad to have another perspective on the issues we faced. He developed a very high level of competence; and I knew that he could deputise for me on occasion if I had to be in two places at once. We did, occasionally, play Mr Nice and Mr Nasty as a way of moving on intransigent situations. We knew there were some of our followers who responded better to him, or better to me – and we played to that. It was a rare interlude where a leader can fully share the burdens, knowing it has the merit of bringing on the next generation.

★★★

Leaders, then, emerge from the whole body of teachers, in a variety of ways and with a myriad aspirations and motivations. Before suggesting some ways in which this initial interest might be captured, something needs to be said about the ground from which they emerge: the teaching profession.

In the space available it is possible only to summarise the bare bones of professionalism as it applies to teaching, but it is important to do so. Leaders in the education system are the people who have the day-to-day oversight of professionalism at the unit level. They need to be aware of how its tentacles reach out into their own work and those of their followers.

The Department for Education (DfE) laid out the bare bones of the issue in a document about teachers' professionalism which covers eight areas within which teachers should operate effectively. They must:

1. Set high expectations that inspire, motivate, and challenge pupils.
2. Promote good progress and outcomes by pupils.
3. Demonstrate good subject and curriculum knowledge.
4. Plan and teach well-structured lessons.
5. Adapt teaching to respond to the strengths and needs of all pupils.
6. Make accurate and productive use of assessment.
7. Manage behaviour effectively to ensure a good and safe learning environment.
8. Fulfil wider professional responsibilities (i.e. towards fellow teachers and parents etc.).

For my part I would add a couple of more detailed provisos which bypass the civil servants. I think that teachers have a duty to teach students to become discerning learners: to have open minds, to collect evidence, to make deductions, to analyse what they are told, and to draw insightful conclusions (incredibly crucial in the electronic age). I was interested to read a research-based article recently which suggested that teachers should rediscover Benjamin Bloom's conceptual structures for education – Bloom put in perspective the teaching of mere information, and demanded that students should be able to analyse, apply, synthesise, and evaluate their knowledge. Decades of government obsession with testing has reduced much so-called knowledge in schools to mere information acquisition. Teachers should take the lead in identifying the fact that most knowledge is interdisciplinary, and that most of the truly great advances in human history have been made outside the constraints of single-subject boundaries[2]. Learning is not a process of limiting but of broadening.

You can read the substance which underpins the DfE dimensions of professionalism at note[3]. The DfE also lays down a wider duty as shown below:

A teacher is expected to demonstrate consistently high standards of personal and professional conduct. The following statements define the behaviour and attitudes which set the required standard for conduct throughout a teacher's career.

- Teachers uphold public trust in the profession and maintain high standards of ethics and behaviour, within and outside school, by:
  o treating pupils with dignity, building relationships rooted in mutual respect, and at all times observing proper boundaries appropriate to a teacher's professional position
  o having regard for the need to safeguard pupils' well-being, in accordance with statutory provisions
  o showing tolerance of and respect for the rights of others
  o not undermining fundamental British values, including democracy, the rule of law, individual liberty and mutual respect, and tolerance of those with different faiths and beliefs
  o ensuring that personal beliefs are not expressed in ways which exploit pupils' vulnerability or might lead them to break the law.
- Teachers must have proper and professional regard for the ethos, policies and practices of the school in which they teach, and maintain high standards in their own attendance and punctuality.
- Teachers must have an understanding of, and always act within, the statutory frameworks which set out their professional duties and responsibilities.

Professional understandings and attitudes inform the activities of teachers and teacher-leaders. What has been said so far identifies what is positive in this process. But if we go back to Angela Thody's description of followership we come up against the less palatable fact that not everything or everyone brings that perspective to their work. Let us, then, look briefly at negative following, since this is a phenomenon which aspirant leaders will encounter.

Angela's collected negative follower-types included:

Machiavellians: slavish and unquestioning followers of leaders who ruthlessly exercise power wherever they can.

Alienates: 'withdraw from leader-follower relationships. They do not join decision making nor support leaders but seldom openly oppose them. They are disgruntled, recognisable as those "muttering" during staff meetings, sitting with arms folded or eyes closed and contributing only such statements as "We tried that before and it didn't work'".

Isolates, passives, dependents, sheep and yes-people: isolates are 'going nowhere', choosing to be virtually outside the organisation; dependents, sheep, and yes-people will only do exactly what they are instructed to do – they opt out of responsibility; passives are 9–5 workers who do not oppose anything nor indicate their support.

Observers: largely passive but may be like the Grand Old Duke of York, who kept his allegiance and options open.

Resisters: tend to oppose the leader with polite statements like: 'with the greatest respect, I have to disagree...'

As you can imagine, the roles these negative staff play are equally unhelpful:

- Distorting communication.
- Acting as saboteurs.
- Creating toxic information or relationships.

I had a saboteur among my staff members. Her ploy was simple. The aim was to destroy my weekends worrying about a crisis that was going to strike on Monday morning. So each Friday, as she left work, Miss Crisis would leave a note for me. As I dealt with my end-of-week messages on Friday afternoon, up would pop an insoluble situation for Monday. The first couple of weeks I was, naturally, quite shaken by this. Then I realised what was happening. So I stopped reading her exquisitely written notes on Friday, and enjoyed my weekends. I was always at work much earlier than her on Monday, and I found ways to obviate the crisis she had attempted to create before she arrived. She never got bored with doing this – even though the ploy had stopped working long ago.

Every community has its fair share of positive people and roles; plus a leaven of the negative. Though the labels are a bit cumbersome, everyone will recognise each of the types described. Aspirant leaders need to face the realism of these positive and negative types of colleague, as well as to learn how to handle both eventualities.

★★★

There are a number of skills and abilities which aspiring and beginning leaders can practise from their earliest days in the profession and which can be used and refined for the remainder of their careers.

- Aspiring or beginning leaders will benefit from a bit of self-analysis. You might look at the positive and negative follower types identified earlier in this chapter to think about your own style as a follower, and how that might inform your understanding when you lead. As a leader, how would you react to each of these follower-styles and what would you do to mitigate the negative ones? Clear-sighted self-analysis is a constant bonus for a leader – we shall return to it in a later chapter.

- Consider your skills as a learner. Do you learn quickly? Do you read quickly (e.g., skim-read or plod through every word – leadership often involves more paperwork)? Can you absorb and retain a lot of information so you don't have to resort to looking things up, which is time-consuming?

- How good are you at timekeeping? This needs to cover not just getting to lessons on time and similar basics; but, how well do you use your time and what skills can you bring to making your approach to tasks time-efficient? A simple thing like arriving at work early means your mind will be in gear for the day ahead; rushing in at the last moment sets the wrong tone and the wrong example.

- Do you communicate and explain well? Are you comfortable talking to your peer group and briefing them? Do you have to write everything down, or can you work from memory or minimal notes? Do you communicate well in both speech and writing?

- Can you conduct meetings? Do you understand the principles of chairing a meeting, producing agendas and Minutes, keeping everyone on task, not letting the most vociferous dominate?

- How persuasive are you? Can you persuade a group of disparate people to your point of view? Are you able to get colleagues who are not otherwise very close to work together amicably and productively? Do you know all your school colleagues, their names, what they do, how they might contribute to your small area of expertise?

- If appropriate, can you work beyond the institution – with parents, with outside professionals, with potential friends of the school?

- Are you a problem-solver? Do you come up with a range of solutions? Can you weigh the relative merits of these solutions to make a sound judgement?
- What is your manner and body-language like? Do you exude confidence? Do you show too much emotion, especially negative emotion?
- Are you fair-minded and able to make decisions impartially and free of staff-room alliances?
- Do you learn from your mistakes, or are you defensive when you get things wrong?
- How do you react to criticism (which may not always be fair) or to advice (even if you choose not to take it)?

One option, if you want to start practising these skills without the pressure of failing in the workplace, is to do so in the outside world; you might become a club secretary, Chair a working group at a charity, or act as events' manager for a local organisation.

What you can't learn but can possess is enthusiasm. You can, however, learn how to convey it to others who follow you. It is not the stuff of speeches (it can be in some circumstances, but more of that later) – it is about action. Lead by example.

Use this section as a checklist to survey your progress in these basic skills over, say, three months. Work on the weaknesses rather than the strengths.

★★★

Contexts alter cases. I was interested to see how leadership compared across different employment sectors and I chose school Heads of Department (HoDs), the hotel and leisure industry's middle managers (HLMs), and the military in the person of Warrant Officers (WOs). The work was very small-scale but it threw up some interesting ideas.

EDUCATION

HoDs were very much orientated to getting the best out of the people for whom they were responsible – both teachers and students. They used various descriptors to illustrate this: 'empowering', 'communicating', and even 'absorbers of stress' in their department members and their managers. But the key concept was undoubtedly 'communication'.

A factor that was central to HoDs was that leadership of department members was harmed by the actions of a small minority of them. Each described a non-conformist among those reporting to them, and HoDs regretted this person could not be easily removed. Non-conformists 'coloured life' in school. One HoD reported that she did not consider herself to be a leader, for she had not ever had any training for leadership: she suggested that actions such as dismissal procedures were the prerogative of those who had.

Conflict with line managers (in all cases a deputy head) was minimal, but if it existed at all it was a private matter expressed away from the other staff. The rare event of conflict was over demands made by senior managers or the senior management team of the school – for example, to cut time for a subject or to cut a budget. In all cases, HoDs claimed their relations with their line managers were good, characterised by critical friendship.

HoDs' declared intentions were to make things better: the delivery of a sound curriculum and a good school experience for students. In selling unpopular decisions to department members they relied on reasoning to explain them or thought it important to empathise with the line manager's point of view. Outside of conflict situations, team working was a key to relationships within the departments.

In terms of a hierarchy within the departments, the HoDs did have people they regarded as deputies, but these individuals essentially 'held the fort' until the HoD was available, rather than dealing directly with situations.

THE MILITARY

The middle managers of the military – the Warrant Officers – who took part in this research did not share the same kind of organisational hierarchy that the HoDs enjoyed. They were, in all cases, relatively long-serving men who reported upwards to younger, middle-ranking officers (major, flight lieutenant). While in schools HoDs were halfway in experience between teachers and their deputy head line managers, in the military the WOs were more experienced than their line managers. They construed their roles as leaders of subordinates and as mentors of their own leaders, therefore. (One even named his officer/manager as one of the team he managed.) Though out-ranked, their advice was taken almost without exception, because it was the voice of experience. Reportedly, 'I wouldn't do that if I were you, sir/ma'am' was usually enough to deflect a bad decision from above.

Nevertheless, the WOs stood in line between officers and troops. They were communicators like the HoDs, but only after they had influenced the message most of the time. It was clear in conversation that any notion of the concept of followership was not being reflected in their words; though the levels of loyalty were significant. One WO made it clear that it was his job to come between bad decisions (though they were rare) from above and the troops below, and this was a shared view.

In terms of subordinates, the conceptual framework of operation was also different from that of the HoDs. Below the WO was a long hierarchy of senior and junior NCOs, and in some cases civilian employees also. The WO's job was described by one as breaking tasks down, to be done, bit by bit and in a logical way, by the people below – in order to achieve the original strategy. Incrementalism and the chain of command were reinforced by the authority of rank, they claimed. There were occasional misfits and awkward customers in the military environment, but if 'would you…' did not produce a result and 'you will' failed as a strategy, then removal was an option and was operationalised.

HOTEL AND LEISURE INDUSTRY

As might have been expected, the HLMs talked a business language: 'Their job (i.e. that of subordinates) is to operationalise part of my business'. This business approach characterised the thinking in three main ways, reported by all respondents. First, it was assumed that everyone, both up and down the hierarchy, had business goals (i.e., the generation of profit) as a key intention by which their jobs were guided. Second, there was a concern for clients, which affected both the choice and the retention of staff. Third, there was a powerful emphasis on teamwork.

These three themes permeated the transcripts generated by each of the HLMs. At times, the implications of the issues became much more far-reaching. For example, our HLM middle managers were responsible for the income generated by the areas of the hotel operation that they controlled – there was considerable accountability.

One of the HLMs spoke in very overt language of total quality management and how the principles of this were applied in the areas for which he was responsible – and, though others were less explicit, the implications were the same. Teams formed substantially because hotel staff worked long and unsocial hours; they were not just thrown together but were dependent on everyone contributing their specific task to the overall operation. Some team members drifted, but poor employees were removed. This had to be done using proper procedures, and might take six months, but the good of the hotel required it.

Our respondents each reported to a General Manager (GM). GMs usually had a traditional hotel background, but some had been off the 'shop floor' for some years. They took a more or less proactive role in the day-to-day running of the hotel, but they were always strategic managers (though the strategy might emanate from company policy). Relations with the GM were good in all cases, and conflict was rare – but these relationships were not described as 'friendships'. Communication in both directions in the hierarchy was critical for HLMs.

Compared with HoDs, HLMs had huge financial responsibilities, and often large human resource responsibilities as well. They were more concerned with removing poor performers from the team, and in this they were closer to the WOs. Hotel teams were closer-knit, perhaps, than teams in most schools, forming social bonds not just a working relationship. Teams were more like those in the military: members had to pull together and guard one another's backs.

★★★

Remember as you start the leadership journey: all leaders have first to have been followers; but not all followers can lead.

Effective leaders are visionaries and innovators. It's an aspiration shared by Miss T, Roy Minton Rhodes, and Denby as they make their way to Britehope Academy – and by YOU, or you wouldn't be reading this book right now. The remaining chapters are intended to throw some light on corners of this worthy aspiration.

2

THE BOOT CAMP OF LEADERSHIP

Nanson maintains that a perfectly folded sock can be a path to greatness

MANAGING   MANAGING > LEADING   SELF-DISCIPLINE

In the previous chapter it has been argued that good leaders in the education sector can emerge only from among those teachers who are fully professional in their approach to teaching as a concept and as a job. In this chapter there is a kind of parallel notion: that good leaders emerge from those who are, first, good managers. Major General Nanson, reviewing the methods of officer cadet leadership training at Royal Military Academy Sandhurst, puts the notion very succinctly, even if in a different context, when he talks of folding socks in the regulation way before inspection, and the gruelling early days of learning to self-manage to the highest standards. But we have to begin with the pedantic bit, by setting down a definition of the difference between management and leadership.

★★★

Various researchers have come up with an important distinction: educational management means the responsibility for the proper functioning of systems within an educational institution; educational leadership is about influencing others to achieve goals.

Having spent time in a department in a university which labelled itself 'Education Management' and whose degree was an MBA, and having transmogrified to one which flew the flag of the International Institute for Educational Leadership and awarded professional doctorates, I became acutely aware that the agendas had changed.

Most of this book is about the leadership element; but this current chapter concerns itself with the rather different business of management: the proper functioning of the system. Learning this skill is the education leader's boot camp.

★★★

Management, then, is about how schools can be made to run smoothly – or in the case of middle leaders, how their areas of responsibility can be run smoothly and contribute to the smooth running of the school. Management is not defined by, but does include, administrative tasks. Teachers (and teacher unions especially) are often resistant to the notion that teachers should carry out routine, administrative, or bureaucratic tasks, but let's not mince words – they are wrong. Any organisation (schools as a whole – but also sub-divisions such as year groups, subject departments, faculties, special groups, and so on) needs a degree of administrative or bureaucratic activity in order to function. Since teachers are often the only people with access to the skills, knowledge, or information to carry out some of the tasks, and are the people with the most need to be aware of the outcomes of them, it makes no sense to espouse a blind policy that every such task should be delegated to someone other than a/the teacher.

The intention of this chapter is to look at the range of management tasks that one might, at some stage in one's career, be asked to perform. Only then can intelligent judgement be made about their usefulness and relevance. When that is accomplished, it will be possible to take a more realistic stance on how leaders, as managers, can cope and what skills they need to do so. As I have emphasised, learning the skills of management is the boot camp of the more refined and agile process of actually leading in school.

Boot camps have a purpose. They are routinely brutal. Yet the name of the game is to inculcate into the sufferer life-saving skills so that, in a crisis, these will become second nature, instinctive; and also so that, at other times, they fall into place naturally and don't take unnecessary energy and cloud the main task (in our case leadership). Passing through this phase (i.e., learning management skills) is important to the acquiring the facility and poise which are the hallmarks of a good leader.

★★★

Teachers carry out a wide range of administrative and management tasks. As they move towards a leadership role the list only expands. Some are confined to the school day, but many of them happen outside school time: that is the nature of the job. In this section we look at the multiplicity of roles a teacher might be engaged in specifically as a manager, rather than as a leader. Remember, managerial tasks are fundamentally about the organisation and its smooth running. Leaders must carry out the managerial elements of their work and then add a leadership layer of activity on top of that. It is therefore important that the management tasks are quickly and efficiently completed. The list below is meant to be indicative not exhaustive; not everyone will do all of these things but there will be some things which are not included here:

IN RELATION TO STUDENTS

Prepare lessons
Write lesson notes
Ensure all required equipment is available and working
Keep the classroom neat, tidy, and fit for purpose
Set up class rules and procedures
Provide a child-safe environment
Perhaps appoint class monitors to undertake helpful jobs
Ensure entry and exit to the room by students is orderly
Devise, adapt, or familiarise one's self with curriculum requirements
Mark work
Provide feedback
Talk with or interview students for specific purposes
Carry out assessment procedures
Record assessment outcomes
Communicate assessment outcomes as appropriate and identify
any problems
Keep attendance records

IN RELATION TO PARENTS

Keep records on students to inform one's knowledge of them
Attend parents' evenings

Give appropriate advice

Contact parents regarding specific problems (depending on school procedures)

Answer queries from parents

Be aware of any particular family circumstances that affect an individual student

Attend School Friends' meetings or events

IN RELATION TO FELLOW STAFF

Brief colleagues appropriately about students and their strengths or problems

Collaborate on curriculum matters

Share staff duties

IN RELATION TO A LINE MANAGER

Keep appropriate records relating to one's appraisal

Seek advice where necessary

Attend appraisal meetings and act on feedback

IN RELATION TO THE HEAD

Promote the ethos of the school

Work in accordance with school norms; for example, about discipline

Report any issues that arise which have more serious implications

Lend support to public events at the school

IN RELATION TO SCHOOL EVENTS

Assist at fundraising events

Use one's skills to provide or promote school productions, concerts, etc.

Participate in extra-curricular activities

Run a club or society

Coach a sport or outdoor activity

IN RELATION TO EXTERNAL BODIES AND ORGANISATIONS

Attend curriculum meetings, such as those organised by exam boards

Liaise with appropriate others – social services, special educational needs, etc.

Brief the school governors on one's area of responsibility

IN RELATION TO CPD

Attend professional courses to promote curriculum, leadership, or other skills

Join a learned society in one's field

Attend events at learned societies

Decide with line manager your CPD priorities

Attend university or other courses or conferences

Gain additional qualifications of value to school and self

Participate in in-house training

Lead an aspect of in-house training

IN RELATION TO IN-HOUSE RESEARCH

Join or lead a group of staff to investigate school-based research issues

Read research literature

Provide feedback to other colleagues

Formulate improved practice following research

Evaluate new practice

IN RELATION TO ORGANISING TEACHING ASSISTANTS

Ensure good relations with teaching assistants

Brief teaching assistants on the roles they need to play each lesson/week

Provide information about relevant students to teaching assistants

Encourage teaching assistants to widen their talents

Where teaching assistants are left to supervise classes, ensure they have all information and materials

IN RELATION TO MENTORING

Help less experienced colleagues on an informal basis
Model good practice for others to follow
Observe colleagues on a mutual-help basis
Provide mentoring feedback to junior colleagues if appropriate
Undertake formal mentoring duties for trainees
Provide careful feedback and positive suggestions for mentees
Liaise with external agencies regarding trainees
Keep good records on mentees and trainees

At all levels of the educational system, management is required; management involves the planning, organising, implementation, review, evaluation, and integration of the processes that support an institution. When you start to manage others, you cross an invisible but real divide. I became acutely aware of that in one new job. On my first day I held a 'getting to know you' meeting for my new staff after the working day. It was a pleasant enough affair. But when it was over and people had dispersed, two colleagues approached me and said: 'You seem like a reasonable boss; but you need to know we will never do anything you ask'. I enquired the reason – could I have upset everyone already? 'Well', they said, 'you have crossed the management divide. From now on it's "them" and "us" – and you are "them"'.

★★★

So what makes a good manager (but also provides a foundation for good leadership)? According to the many business-orientated articles that find their way onto the internet there are countless characteristics that are needed. But the flaw with this is that the writers confuse managing with leading. We have seen that management is really about the routine or emergent activities that keep the institution (or some part of it, like a year group or subject area) running effectively. As a result, I have kept my list of essential management characteristics down to a dozen – and these are designed to be the backdrop and context to leadership.

Ideally, managers should:

BE WELL BRIEFED AND KNOWLEDGEABLE

Good management is promoted by a manager who is well-briefed and knowledgeable. The opposite of this results in the proverbial situation of 'the blind leading the blind'. If they don't know, good managers take pains to find out. Good managers have experience of the school situation; they have 'been there before' (even if not as managers); they can thus ensure the right things happen in the right ways and reassure other colleagues. This does not mean that good managers will be fixated on the past, but they will have the perspicacity to use past knowledge to inform the present and future.

HAVE A CALM TEMPERAMENT

Keeping any organisation working well happens when the manager has a clear head and a steady hand. The manager's job is to hold the institution's course, and to allay the fears of those around them. Some organisations seem not to work in this way – they lurch from one crisis to another and, if there isn't a crisis, they want to create one!

As a manager I always tried to stay calm – listen first, weigh the problem, evaluate between all possible solutions, come to a measured conclusion, avoid drama. One morning a member of staff had indicated she wanted to talk to me. She was an exceptionally clever and well-qualified individual with, as far as I could judge, a positive self-image. There was a curriculum problem caused by the change of rubrics by an Examination Board and we talked it through. I think I helped her to reach her own solution: it was a question of managing the change by adapting the way parts of the subject were taught. At the end we chatted generally and in an informal manner for a few minutes about how her work was progressing. I thought this conversation was coming to an end, but suddenly she remarked, 'Some of us, you know, find you very difficult to work with'. Things had suddenly become more serious. I asked her why she felt this. 'Well', she said, 'our previous boss used to shout at us if anything didn't go smoothly, and you don't. That's very hard. We don't know where we stand'.

You can predict some of the ensuing dialogue – about professionalism, valuing people, and so on. But I was quite shaken by this remark: not that she (and others) might think I was failing in some way, but that they would think the solution was being bawled out.

HAVE POSITIVE ATTITUDES

This is a tricky one – but positivity comes from enjoying what you do and, in a team, from other people enjoying what they do. As a manager it is possible to contribute to the context in which others can be positive and behave positively – but, when the chips are down, you can't make another person positive. For some, the glass is always half empty; but a manager can exude positive vibes, help others to see the good side of any situation, have relaxed body language, and encourage success. On one occasion my management team and I were faced with a crisis brought about by a change of Government policy. The issues were long-term and serious, and we needed to take stock. I arranged for them to get off-site, and I booked a room in a small local hotel. The conference room was cosy, in what one would have called an attic, and looked out onto an idyllic view. We spent a day thrashing out the problems as we saw them: the morning was dedicated to everyone having their full and frank say on the matter with all ideas considered, no decisions only expression of viewpoints. The afternoon was designed for members of the management team to write sections of a joint outcomes paper. In the end (as so often happens) things changed – with governments they usually do – but the paper that resulted from the day became locally famous as 'The Attic Paper', was published, and became something of a position statement.

BE FLEXIBLE

If possible, I like to find several solutions to a problem, and offer people the chance to choose between them – that's the ideal, it doesn't always work, but it's worth striving for. The trouble with fixedness is that it becomes a trap for one's self not just the other parties involved. In one school I worked in we were experiencing a series of very cold winter days; I dreaded going to supervise in the playground where normally I would not have bothered with a coat. The head was a bit of an outdoors man, and he found a lot of students inside the building at lunchtime. The next day he issued a blanket decree that NO ONE would be inside the school during the lunchbreak unless eating their meal.

At morning break a student (not one of my class, though I taught him) approached me and said: 'Please can I stay in your classroom at lunchtime?' I told him no – there was a head's directive and neither he nor I could break it. But he was distressed; eventually I said to him that I understood his concern as I felt the cold too, but I couldn't see an option. He said something very poignant then: 'If I go outside, I will die'. To cut a long story short, David had no coat (didn't own one), was very poor, his jacket was ill-fitting, his shirt was threadbare; to cap it all, he was very skinny and hardly ate. He had confided in me; maybe he should have gone to the head, but he was obviously reluctant.

I decided I couldn't betray his trust, so I came to an agreement:

> I have some marking to do at lunchtime. You can come to my room but, if anyone challenges you, you say that you are doing an urgent cataloguing job on some new books in the class library that the teacher wants to loan out.

There was a collection of new books but it was a feeble story even though it worked. It was even feebler because David went for specialist remedial reading one a week, so allegedly he couldn't read let alone catalogue!

While he pretended to catalogue, I noticed he was actually looking at something under the desk. It turned out to be a radio, hand-built, which he had made from a kit from instructions in a magazine. 'But you can't read', I said – and he laughed. 'OK', I said, 'from now on when I give the class a reading and writing task you do it too instead of just scribbling nonsense'. He did.

BE POLITICALLY ASTUTE

Politics come with big P's and little p's. Because education is funded by the taxpayer the big P of politics is something to which we all need to be sensitive, but there are also the smaller p's of in-school relationships: colleagues who try to avoid one another because of some historical antagonism; a head who believes that Ofsted should be subverted whenever possible; a colleague who spreads gossip about others. Being politically astute keeps the manager out of the danger zone and helps to ease the decisions he/she has to make.

USE TIME EFFECTIVELY

Managers are the gatekeepers of time. There is more on this topic in Chapter 8, but for the moment, let it just be noted that there are ploys in one's personal life that can expand one's time as a manager: thinking out a difficult problem on the daily train commute; making lists so that tasks are not forgotten; taking time out to recharge the batteries.

MAKE TIME FOR PEOPLE AND SHOW RESPECT

At this point, the issue of making time for people – staff or students – is more important. A manager often claims that 'my door is always open'. We all know that should read: 'always open except when it's closed'. But there are ways of keeping the door open, like simply being habitual – letting everyone know you are always at work by 7.45 and will be in your office and ready to answer any queries. Making time for your fellows is a sign of respect for them, and colleagues tend to respond to that. It signals care, and a proper professional organisation. Good managers treat everyone – staff, support personnel, students, and parents – with equal politeness and good manners.

COMMUNICATE WELL

Good managers communicate effectively. They say what they mean and do it succinctly and with clarity. In that way they share the mission of the department, school, etc. They also leave little room for ambiguity, so that colleagues understand that, while 'we are all in it together', nonetheless they have a responsibility which is shared both up and down the school hierarchy.

HAVE OR ACQUIRE TECHNICAL CAPABILITY

New electronic means have opened up many possibilities in school. Records can be collected and stored electronically, which (if staff are properly trained) can speed up the process. Older colleagues need to be made aware that rejecting these methods as 'new tricks' is no defence. We have an obligation to use all the best means to work seamlessly with one another. A recent article talked about alternative means of feedback to students. Students submitted work electronically in a personal OneNote classroom area and their feedback from the teacher was added through audio or video-recording. Students were obliged to watch/listen to this, and to respond. Many other tasks can be streamlined in these kinds of ways: from writing e-mails rather than letters to communicating with external agencies.

BE EFFICIENT

Efficiency includes not only doing a good job in good time but thinking about what will make the outcome of that job more effective for others. If the outcome of your work is a paper, maybe keep it brief, write it in bullets, sequence it logically, clarify what actions need to be taken by whom in what timescale. If a graph or a diagram tells the story more effectively, use those means. Don't waste everyone's time by sending circulars, such as e-mails to people who don't need to know the subject matter – quicker for you maybe, a waste for them. Don't ever indulge in a professional context in those time-consuming social messages that relate to people most have never met – what I call 'Rosemary's baby messages'.

BE THOROUGH AND SYSTEMATIC

Cross all the t's and dot all the i's of a job first time round. Doing the same job again because a step has been omitted is a waste of your time and other people's.

PROVE A LOW KEY, AUTHORITATIVE PRESENCE

Finally, try to be the kind of person others believe can and will complete jobs, solve problems, and advise them effectively. Education managers must solve real-world problems that impinge on both the staff they lead, and the students whose lives are affected. For example, how might you deal with this:

Arguably, one of the best ways of persuading students to obey rules is to encourage them to participate in devising them. While you are happy with this, a member of your team is violently opposed, arguing that this is a diminution of the teacher's professional status and a route to laxity. How might you intervene in these objections to defuse the situation?

It might be worth adding here that, onerous though the management duties are, it is possible and right sometimes to draw a line in the sand. Many, many demands flood in on managers. These must be prioritised. Sometimes a job will simply get put on the bottom of the pile until it becomes irrelevant. From time to time the manager may just have to say: 'No. It is not a key element in my workload'. There is no shame in 'No' if it's justified.

★★★

So, the first step on the road to genuine leadership is to be an effective manager – someone who can make things happen and take others along too. From what has been said, you can work out the key qualities that managers need and which form the covert basis of leadership skill:

- Be authoritative: know your stuff and keep up to date in your field – expertise provides a level of self-confidence and brings out confidence in others.
- Be a role model: don't ask others to do what you can't or won't do yourself.
- Be a good communicator: explain clearly what the task is and how to reach the goal – avoid the pitfalls of jargon and obscurity.
- Know how to take decisions: weigh the situation carefully, but when you know what the way forward has to be, be decisive and convey the decision crisply.
- Be positive: keep the team interested and buoyant.
- Hone your emotional intelligence: you have to understand people in order to manage them, even more so to be an effective leader.
- Be honest: don't flannel to soften the blow of your reality or what needs to be done if it is unpopular. Explain the necessity and then bite the bullet.
- Above all, be a person of integrity: don't just tell the truth, be someone who can be relied on to explore the most professional and ethical answer to a problem.

Leaders get into some tricky situations: external constraints like finance bite into their work; colleagues sometimes fail and let the team down; a head might become sick and leave the school rudderless for a time. The cadre of skills leaders have learned as managers will keep the show on the road and give them the breathing-space to lead. We shouldn't, as leaders, try to escape from the tricky bits. Grass may not be greener over the fence, it may just be attracting more sunlight. A cynical view, but apt!

When Major General Nanson speaks of the folded sock he is making just this point. An officer in the field needs to ensure that they have, first and foremost, looked after the basics: they have the right equipment in the bergen, suitable rations, the rifle is clean and functioning – that they are self-managing. Self-management imposes self-discipline and a sense of pride: but 'only once you have your own house in order can you help the men and women under your leadership to do the same', says the General. Secure in *self-discipline* you can then be free to go on and lead – to influence *others* on a mission towards better professional practice. This simple truth is a fundamental life lesson, too. That's where we are going in the following chapters, knowing that our socks are folded and our kit will function.

3

THINKING IN A CRISIS
Panic destroys reasoned thought

SUCCESS & FAILURE   STRESS   RESILIENCE   CONFIDENCE

Fear elicits strange reactions. When the blackbird in your garden spots a cat, rather than instantly flying away (which would seem prudent), it may indulge in what is known as displacement behaviour. In other words, instead of taking decisive action to quit the scene, it stands around and does something 'off the wall' like defecating or picking up seeds. Humans under stress can be guilty of similar dissonant reactions: the chemicals produced by fear make us act irrationally and there is a good chance we will lose control. Under attack or in a crisis, we panic.

In the previous chapter it was suggested that one form of defence is to form excellent habits and mind-sets that make us less vulnerable, and this is indeed good advice. But no one can control what may happen in a live situation. Looking so early in the book at what might go wrong on the leadership journey is important for two reasons: first, eventually something will; second, you need to be ready for the cold surge of fear when it does. Often, texts on being a leader omit to tackle this most emotive of subjects; but that's cowardice. In Chapter 1 we discovered that the leadership journey often begins among people who have none of the necessary preparation for the role, and in Chapter 2 it was pointed out that the boot camp of managing would provide us with the critical skill of self-discipline, which would underpin our eventual leadership abilities. This, then, is the correct psychological moment to deal with failure.

★★★

One of the insights that I gained over my time as a manager and a leader sounds simplistic but is extremely important: Every silver lining has its cloud just as every cloud has its silver lining. By this I meant that however good things seem at this moment, the bubble will burst, so be happy that things are indeed good right now, but don't get complacent (or even, in some circumstances, let your guard down). Conversely, from time to time the world will seem black, but most situations, however apparently awful, turn out to have a compensation – you just need to look for it.

If you think about it, should the Ofsted inspectors report on a Friday night that the school has been rated outstanding and there are no flaws that need urgent attention, that is a moment of satisfaction and rejoicing for all involved. But, come Monday morning, everything could be stood on its head as a result of vandalism or accident to the school plant over the intervening weekend. The following quotation from a study of school-based fires by the National Foundation for Education Research[1] sums up the issue:

> In the secondary school, the fire had occurred during the Christmas holidays and had destroyed the entire Physical Education department. This had been the second major fire that the school had suffered, with the previous one, three years earlier, having damaged a large part of the school (the previous fire had been the result of an arson attack). At the other primary school the fire, which had occurred on a Saturday afternoon, and again had spread through the roof space, destroyed the library, IT suite and a nurture unit, and further fire and water damage had made other areas unusable.

The trauma of this kind of event would be massive (with or without Ofsted). Even less serious traumas can be disruptive. But the opposite is also true: what seems like a small tragedy at the time might well turn out to be a blessing.

A fellow leader, a department head in a similar organisation to my own, told me she had had a problem in one of her courses. The course leader had put on a display of work at an Open Day, and it was very impressive. However, a parent had spotted that some pieces of the work had students' names on them – and they were names of students who had left the course some time ago. There was little doubt the items were being touted as evidence of current achievement by the course staff. The upshot had been a show-down between the head of department and the long-term course leader where it became clear that corners had been cut. The head of department treated the matter very seriously; she arranged retraining for the course leader and demanded close scrutiny of his work for a period thereafter. At first the course leader complied, but then became uncooperative and refused to remodel his behaviour; on being pressed, he resigned. The course team members were quite shaken, but also a bit concerned that they might be tarred with the same brush. The resignation even reached the local Press: the course leader had been a well-known figure in the local community and there was a certain amount of backlash from members of the community who were associated with the work. However, a new course leader was appointed and brought a fresh and dynamic approach to the work. Both staff and students flourished in the new regime. The head of department's action was justified in the changes for the better which ensued.

Most experienced leaders are agreed: leaders are distinguished from managers by the fact that they innovate as opposed to just keeping the organisation running (albeit efficiently); and they take difficult decisions in the process of innovation. But leadership involves risk, not every innovation works, mistakes will be made. That fact in turn demands from leaders very specific characteristics. You can also rely on the fact that everyone will blame you.

★★★

Leaders need the high degrees of self-discipline and self-knowledge referred to in the previous chapter. But beyond that they need mental toughness: what is now often referred to as resilience. Resilience is 'the process of adapting well in the face of adversity, trauma, tragedy, threats or significant sources of stress'[2]. There are famous examples, of course, such as Dame Tanni Grey-Thompson (wheelchair Olympian and now Welsh Assembly politician and vice-chancellor of a university) and Welsh Guardsman Simon Weston (who survived the *Sir Galahad* attack in the Falklands to have a media career and be a major player in charity fundraising).

The ultimate outcome of failing to show resilience is often quoted as suicide. A recent survey suggested that teachers have a suicide rate about 30 per cent above the national average. Statistics, however, can be misleading. Not all these suicides will be school-trauma related, and we can't tell what the proportions are from the figures. In the same way, we hear a great deal in the media about suicides among former military personnel – and the figures would suggest that these might run at about the same level as those of teachers. But then, it is a surprise, perhaps, to discover that dentists too have high suicide rates. Is there a connection? Probably, and the link seems to be that professionals have higher rates than those in non-professional occupations. So we have to be careful about portraying teaching as a super-stressful profession. Nonetheless, education leaders are as subject to crisis, stress, failure, depression, inability to cope as are other people in comparable jobs.

The road back from trauma or failure is not easy: learning to be resilient is likely to involve considerable emotional distress but we can all learn increased resilience. Frequently, while they can be helped by the presence of a supportive team, those who find their resilience go through specific stages:

- making realistic plans for the next step;
- retaining a positive view of self;
- showing doggedness in problem-solving;
- controlling strong feelings, emotions and responses to the situation or other people.

The resilient leader is a successful leader who exhibits these characteristics: he or she avoids seeing crises as insurmountable problems; accepts or welcomes change; redefines the goals when necessary; acts decisively to alleviate the situation.

Even relatively untraumatic failures draw out important resilience features in successful leaders, such as the ability to face unwelcome messages; the skill of keeping a clear head in what for others is a crisis; the willingness to back themselves when things are uncertain; the openness to listen and accept support or ideas. But the key quality is tolerance of ambiguity, to carry on even when the path is obscure and the end of the journey can't be guaranteed.

One important quality in a leader, should they be subject to some failed enterprise, is just to be able to stand back and say, 'Sorry. I got it wrong. Let's move on'. Honesty, which is the first step on the road to integrity, is usually respected by those around, and may even be a rallying point for followers.

★★★

There is one further important set of actions that you can take as a leader, sometimes during, but certainly following, a failed enterprise: stop, take stock, give yourself breathing space, replan, pick out the good bits.

Leaders who can't do these things fall prey to stress. A recent *Guardian* article reported that the education sector was at breaking point, with teachers twice as anxious as the general population and with overwork the norm[3]. The future, it suggested, would be burnout for leaders on a massive scale. The reason, it was alleged, was a combination of too much paperwork, accountability, and the fact that teachers no longer feel trusted.

I don't want to underplay this at all, and I can certainly think of a few stressed-out teachers and leaders. We are all being asked to give more thought to mental health, and how to stay fit in situations that stress us. But what has been said in this chapter is important: all life contains setbacks; setbacks produce stress; there are ways to lessen the impact of that on ourselves and those around us; we have a responsibility to ourselves to act in a way that de-stresses us and others, or holds stress at bay.

One critical piece of advice is to take appropriate breaks (time management will help in this – see Chapter 8), but it isn't just a case of not being at work. The successful leader has to learn to switch off. For my part, I found that I could work up to, quite literally, the last moment when a vacation was due – I would ensure that every last job was crossed off my list, but then I could shut off my mind completely, and concentrate on being on vacation. At the other end of the process I packed away the suitcase and the following morning went back to work ready to tackle the next (exciting) set of problems and challenges.

If you cannot de-stress in the ways suggested throughout this book – i.e. by acting in your leadership role without undue pressure and by de-stressing yourself – then you may need to seek professional help and you should do so before the pressure builds up too much. It may be that a spell away from leadership is right for you, or that using your talents in another way is more appropriate. We have to be realistic about ourselves. The contemporary writer Alexander McCall Smith encapsulates this realism in a brief sentence which suggests we are all capable of a masterpiece if the canvas is small enough. McCall

Smith's whimsical humour often catches the mood of the human condition; for leaders, ambition is a good thing, over-ambition is a destructive force.

Major General Nanson paints a leadership picture that accords with my experience:

> Remaining calm as a leader, especially when you find yourself in hot water, requires a level of mental resilience – but when you stay calm others will be calmed too. Likewise, a display of panic will be reflected back in the behaviour of your team… give yourself a second and let your mind catch up.

★★★

One of the messages of the chapter so far is about self-knowledge: knowing our strengths and weaknesses, knowing our limitations. But it is also about building on the limitations and weaknesses to become stronger and more effective. How can we begin to make this self-analytical journey?

One extremely simple yet very effective tool is to keep a reflective log of things that happen in your leadership life. You might record the major events of the day in the form of a diary; or you might log only things that are 'critical incidents' in your thinking. Critical incidents are events that perhaps cause you at least to pause and maybe to struggle at the time, and which have the potential to inform how your leadership thinking might change. Either kind of recording is valuable, it's really a matter of preference.

The following is an example of a segment from a reflective log kept by a leader:

> Today we had an incident of theft – very rare. I had been given a small grant to establish a year-group library for Year 9; the team had chosen some exciting titles. The books looked new and inviting. The caretaker had assembled a shelf-unit to house them; the volumes were all piled up on a side table ready to be classified into sections like fiction, biography, wildlife and so on. But when I went to arrange them, I realised that two titles were missing – both Harry Potters. We looked everywhere, but no one knew where they were. There hadn't been any actual lessons in the room since the books were piled up, but a lot of students – Year 9 and others – had come to and fro legitimately. The team was very angry and wanted to make maximum public fuss about

it. The head thought she might talk about it in assembly. I was undecided: there was no positive evidence they had been stolen even though they were missing; and making a lot of noise about the incident could have negative effects both on students who might want to borrow books from the new collection, and it might give other students ideas they didn't previously harbour. In the end, the head and the team left the decision to me.

Whether you choose the diary format, or the collection of critical incidents, once the material is collected it needs to be analysed. This can be done by you alone; or in collaboration with a mentor. At this point you need to interrogate the records you have kept. The pro forma (Table 3.1) suggests a possible way of doing this, but the

Table 3.1 Pro forma for interrogating your diary or log

What happened?
Who was involved?
What was the fundamental problem?
What role did you play?
What effective words or action did you use?
What ineffective behaviour did you exhibit?
How was the incident resolved?
To what extent was the resolution satisfactory?
What parts of the resolution were unsatisfactory?
What would you do differently if you were to replay the incident?
What have you learned about the situation described?
What have you learned about the other people involved?
As a person
What have you learned about yourself?
As a leader?
Can you sum up the major learning point from this incident in one sentence?

whole process can be malleable and adapted to your own needs and preferences.

The analytical journal is a great tool but is probably most effective when used sparingly: for example, for a couple of weeks to see what you discover about your leadership; during a time of particular pressure; as a working document when you want to further your skills about specific issues.

The late Clive James, academic, poet, professional traveller and observer of the human condition, in his *Unreliable Memoirs*, talks about surfing in his native Australia and sums up the panic that set in when he failed to surf a wave. As leaders we know we can't walk on water, only when it freezes (as Beyoncé says). Sometimes, we catch the freezing moment and surprise ourselves.

★★★

In the end, it all comes down to one word: confidence. Good leaders are confident they can handle setbacks, even the occasional failure; as well as realistically confident they can handle success.

4

ONLY THE BEST – ADOPTING A QUALITY STANDARD
The swagger stick of leadership

QUALITY   VISION   MISSION   SELF-BELIEF

I used to collect small examples of antique photographica: silver-point prints, 3D cards, and *cartes-de-visite*, those little pictures of wallet size that were put in albums by collection-obsessed Victorians and Edwardians. Among these *cartes-de-visite*, and probably the most recent of their kind, were portraits of soldiers about to go off to war in 1914. They were usually taken in formal set-ups in the studio of the local photographer, often with a small table or some other prop. But the photographer wanted to make his subjects look as smart and imposing as possible, so he would make them hold a swagger stick: a short cane often with a silver top. In the military the swagger stick was, and is, usually used by senior NCOs or officers, but the photographer understood its value. The person holding it cannot but stand up taller and straighter, chest out, stomach in, head held high, looking proud. He wanted his subjects to look their best, to be outstanding, and this simple ploy worked. When you look like a winner, you often win.

What would your *carte-de-visite* say about you as a leader? Where do you want to be on the leadership continuum? Poor, adequate, competent, good, outstanding? Most of us don't make outstanding whatever we turn our hands to, but we can be good and aspiring higher.

★★★

What follows in this chapter has the intention of helping to articulate a personal approach or philosophy to underpin your personal leadership journey. Having looked so far in this text at how we got to be leaders, at developing self-discipline, at using that self-discipline to handle ourselves when in a crisis, we could use one short phrase to summarise the theme, the quality of our performance. Performance is a concept that can be applied at both institutional and individual levels.

At an institutional level, the focus has been to investigate and identify the characteristics of high-performing institutions so that they can be inculcated into lower performing ones: the outcomes are things to recognise as desirable and to which the lower performers can aspire. Research was, and is, directed at finding these 'magic ingredients' of excellence so that they could be applied elsewhere: the movement is generally known as the 'improving schools movement'[1].

Are the findings of the unfolding improving schools research useful? The most honest answer to this question is equivocal: yes and no. In the early days, much of the research came up with lists of characteristics of improving schools, which typically contained items like:

- Effective school leadership.
- Shared vision or mission.
- High standards for students.
- Curriculum aligned with national requirements.
- Teaching and learning monitored regularly.
- Supportive environment for students.
- Staff involved in professional development.
- School involved in the community.

There's nothing wrong with any of these items, but one might make three pertinent observations about this approach. First, it does seem to be stating the blindingly obvious. Second, there are no definitions of key words like 'effective' or 'high standards'. Third, enthusiastic researcher-practitioners went off to their respective countries to try either to generate lists like this from studying 'good' schools, or they took the ill-defined categories and applied them to other institutions to identify where they were not performing up to standard. The trouble was, there was incomplete consistency of methodology, and so – far too often – what emerged was little more than platitude, and at best a goal with no path towards it.

The approach also smacks too much of the business model of quality: The use of numerical models by which to assess the performance of an organisation, its component parts or employees, through the use of statistics, measurements or surveys, with a view to making judgements about quality. With 'measurement' now at the heart of education, teachers and middle leaders had to be assessed or appraised.

On the individual level, the system works like this: line managers carry out conversations (appraisals) that are intended to result in target-setting for the follower. Line manager (appraiser) and follower (appraisee) agree a set of target outcomes and a timescale for completion; the appraisee's performance is reviewed against the targets at the end of the designated period. This process, it is claimed, provides a 'measure' of performance. (It can, of course, include actual measures such as numbers of students reaching designated levels in SATs or GCEs.) The line manager is, in turn, appraised by a more senior manager – and so on, hierarchically, throughout the organisation.

I, like many educationists, get very irritable when we have the world of business and business models constantly thrust at us by the government and the public as exemplars of good practice and systems to be emulated. Take just one trivial example. Over the course of any one day, tens of thousands of teachers teach hundreds of thousands of lessons, almost none of them fail to run to time. Yet, when I tried to book my routine boiler service in good time for its due date in September, I was informed that, despite the TV adverts, the first available appointment would be in January of the following year! A school that ran, even for a day, to that level of efficiency would fail, it would dissolve into anarchy. But surely, performance management is a good thing?

★★★

The analysis of performance – the individual's and the institution's – must be an important tool in raising both levels of competence and aspirations. Rather than appraisal, I prefer to think in terms of accountability. As a teacher it is my responsibility to teach interesting lessons, to keep students safe, to achieve excellent examination results, to bring every child on to the highest achievement possible, to support the ethos of the school. As a leader, I am accountable to pursue the school's mission within my own context, lead my team to that end, draw out the individual skills within the team, hand opportunities to others, and so on.

So, if 'measurement' in the business sense is often sterile when translated into the education system, what can be taken from this performance process that is positive? What can an education leader do in order to make themselves and their followers more effective? What marks out the leader's personal quality in his/her role?

There can be little doubt the starting point is in your own psychology: to be inspiring, you have to be inspired; to motivate others, you yourself have to be motivated. True motivation comes from within. It probably depends on a number of 'habits of mind':

- Know what your aims and intentions are (write them down so that you don't get deflected).
- Identify your values.
- Don't be deflected from either your intentions or your values.
- Always be positive, and help others around you to think positively.
- Choose positive people as role models and mentors.
- Eradicate negative attitudes ('we tried it before and failed'; 'we can't afford it').
- Travel to your goals incrementally, don't expect to arrive in one leap.
- Celebrate the successful steps on the route.
- Make good relations with your team of followers.
- Trust, delegate to, and reward your followers when they too take small steps.
- Reinforce the notion of 'being in it together' or collegiality.
- Know when to take a break to renew your energy.

This is a true story about positivity:

Part of one of my jobs was to run a multi-million-pound budget. Claiming the money and spending it were each hedged around with a complete rulebook of provisos and roadblocks. My finance assistant was brilliant at knowing and implementing the rules, but I, and the teachers who depended on the money, were frustrated that the rules got in the way of intelligent decisions to spend it and depressed the benefits it had for its intended recipients. One day I sat down with my assistant and said:

You are good at these rules, and I value having someone who can ensure that I don't break any of them. But could we invent a different approach? How about finding the ways in which I *can* spend the money and still stay within the official guidance? The process of doing this would be quite intellectually challenging for you, but the rewards would be hugely appreciated by our clients.

The finance assistant thought about this for a little while, and then said: 'We'll give it a try'. They did. It worked.

★★★

In Chapter 1 we established the principle that effective leaders, in striving for the best, would generate a vision for their work (Chapter 7 will expand on this theme). For the moment, take it as read that the first step towards quality in leadership is to develop a quality vision or mission: to know what you want. Then you have to move on: how do you get it? What does a quality leader do to implement a quality vision? They must communicate the vision, and that is not so easy at it sounds.

A high-flying colleague of mine took over as head of a very difficult and run-down primary school in a deprived area. They were massively self-motivated, with a fine ability to formulate the mission to transform the school – even to put that vision into words. This was a young professional of rare skill. They asked me if they could come and rehearse with me their first speech to the staff, to be delivered in a staff meeting at the end of their first day in office. I was more than happy to listen, even to give advice, which could be taken or left. My colleague came, and the speech was superb: a pertinent vision, persuasively worded, and educationally sound, emotionally appealing. It took a full hour to deliver. By the end I was very disheartened. I made some key points which I felt were valid:

- The talk was well aimed and on target; but definitely too much, too soon.
- The staff had been demoralised for months; they would not rise to total enthusiasm in one hour.
- The mission was clear but the steps on the path were not.
- The route to a new era demanded massive time commitment from the head – but also from a staff whose readiness was not yet tested; they were worn out with failure.

- Miracles happen, but realism is necessary to take others along the path.
- As a leader, one must take others with you: you can't do it all yourself, the workload will grind you to a pulp.

I suggested a major rethink. The advice was ignored. Staff queued up to leave. The new head did not stay the academic year. It took a huge personal toll.

★★★

Are there any techniques which can be used to improve, sustain, and communicate quality as your hallmark without mentally exhausting either you or your followers? The answer is affirmative, and probably includes some, or all, of these factors:

- At the risk of being repetitive (but it is critical) you, as leader, must have a vision, and the vision has to be articulated into a clear mission statement which is persuasive and communicated in a way that fires others' enthusiasm, too. As well as the mission, there has to be a delineated journey by which to travel to it: a strategy, with long-term and short-term goals.
- The leader has to take the team along, as we have said; achieving the vision has to seem realistic to them, and within their capabilities. They need to feel your trust and to share the enterprise – this is critical. They need to know that you will listen to their concerns even though you will not deviate from the core purpose.
- But you need to communicate the fact that you will lead, and that means that you will take decisions, and the responsibility for those decisions. Make sure that your public face is one of decisiveness. If you are not happy on the front line, then leadership is not for you.
- When you make a leadership decision, examine your motives for it. Remember, the great virtue of a teacher-professional is integrity.
- Know your followers well: play to their strengths and ensure that their weaknesses are supported by you or by someone else. Encourage those with leadership potential to use it for the common ends. If colleagues have potential as leaders, ensure their skills are trained and practised. Make sure your emerging

lieutenants know that, if they make an error through inexperience, you will take the responsibility and protect them.
- Void the comments of the doom-raisers, but don't allow over-optimism, which may lead to failure and disappointment.

***

Learning the art of sustained motivation in self and others is not easy; it may be one of the hardest things a leader has to do. The temptation is always to feel 'everything falls on my shoulders'. That's actually because it does, and there's no way around that. It is what makes some people so-called 'natural leaders' (an inaccurate and misleading description) and makes others shy away from responsibility. Pundits suggest that there are probably three factors that make good leaders persevere:

- The first is autonomy – confidence in one's self and one's actions, a clear sense of purpose and the ability to articulate one's goals.
- Second is a security which is built on personal values – knowing what is right, being willing to stand up for that and go the extra mile.
- Third, there is increasing competence – a sense of security is often based on sound knowledge, careful preparation, and careful weighing of risks, all of which happen if you feel knowledgeable and informed.

To these three commonly cited characteristics, I would add innovation – a desire and confidence to invent new things and new ways of doing things; not change for change's sake, but an openness to give alternative approaches an evaluation. You could use jargon phrases here (beloved of the business world) like 'blue-sky thinking', or 'thinking outside the box', but let's keep it simple.

Sustaining motivation in others is partly by example: no one follows an insecure, shoulders-sagging doubter, after all. Continuous improvement in others should be as valued in them as in one's self. The effective leader may prefer collegiality to criticism (though, on occasions, one just has to be blunt). The leader values the interest others have in their work, and the professional development they sustain to improve their performance. These 'others' (team members, followers) need appropriate empowerment to begin to take their leadership steps, too.

Many leaders (and others) fear external scrutiny; my advice is – use it even if you don't accept all of it as valid. You or your team might benefit from the words of a mentor, from the work of a consultant, from a session of in-house or external professional development, or from a formal inspection process. Make positive use of critiques, but be critical of them, too.

In one of my roles it was announced that an HMI would be visiting us in a few days' time. I agreed to drive to the local station to meet him. My deputy was filled with a mixture of delight and fear. Delight that 'certain colleagues' would get found out; fear (I suspect) that it might be him! As I left for the station, he said: 'You look so relaxed. How can you be relaxed at a time like this?' My reply surprised him, I think:

> On the way from the train I will give him a run-down of our strengths and weaknesses because I know them far better after six months than HMI can after two days. He'll look to see if I'm right. His analysis and mine will end up along the same lines. But when he says it, it will strengthen my hand to act and over-come resistance to the necessary changes. For me, it can only be win–win.

★★★

The import of this chapter is about creating a climate of excellence and quality as a result of your leadership, not least your leadership of learning (curricular or extra-curricular). Excellence is achieved, to a large extent, through the quality of the act of teaching, not in the information conveyed. To this end you might consider the following questions in relation to your leadership of learning:

Ensuring that students learn using a variety of methodologies is likely to be the most successful approach to inclusivity in learning. To what extent, and how, do you monitor how the teaching staff you lead use a variety of learning methods: quality didactic teaching, insightful questions, expansion of curiosity, use of learning technologies, visitors and visits, interdisciplinary understanding, and so on? What practical and ethical problems arise with each of these methods? What can you, as a leader of learning, do about the problems?

In your area of responsibility as a leader there are characteristics that should never be compromised. Followers in your team should share your intentions and your commitment to them. But they should do so because these same followers should feel content working in a supportive emotional climate: strength in support. The students should be encouraged to share in and support the climate: good class management should be matched by good discipline. In too many educational settings, potentially effective learning is undermined by poor student behaviour. Deal with the basics before you add the frills to maximise students' time-on-task.

All the learning experiences should contribute to making learning interesting and keeping students engaged. The intellectual climate should allow for students to think; that is, to ask questions, to seek clarification, even to ask for justifications for statements made. Education should be challenging (but behaviour should never be – an important distinction). Desmond Morris had it right in his view of life: 'The trick is never to stop asking questions and never stop exploring, whether it is new places or new ideas'. Talk between staff members, and between students, and between students and staff should flow naturally and be a feature of the creative atmosphere that is nurtured.

In the following true account, you as the leader should ask yourself about the nature of the leadership at work in the school described, and how it impinged on students' learning:

> I was engaged in trying to establish what skills teachers needed to make students articulate and of independent thought. I had come to the view that a major trigger in this was not feeding students information, but in asking them questions and engaging them in open-ended discussion. To pursue the matter further I asked one Local Authority to nominate an 'expert teacher' in this field whom I could interview in depth.
>
> On the due day I met and interviewed the nominated teacher, I was delighted to sit in on his exciting lessons with high-contributing students. Then it was break-time. We went to the staffroom. I took my coffee and went to sit among the staff group; but he quickly guided me away into a corner. I asked him if it was something I had done. 'No', he said. 'You see, I encourage the students not to accept things at face value; but when they go to other lessons they carry on in the same vein. This upsets my colleagues, so they have isolated me as a pay-back. They want a quiet life, not challenge'.

★★★

This chapter has been about quality. It is unrepentantly about quality, though there is a *caveat* here about aiming to do the best. It is not the job of leadership to push others (staff or students) beyond what is reasonable in the circumstances, still less to jeopardise their mental or physical health in pursuit of a personal ambition. Getting the best out of people is not an excuse for driving them into the ground for personal aggrandisement. However, at this point it must also be said that there is an element of our society which has rewritten the English language to eliminate notions such as 'best', 'quality', 'competition', 'success', 'winning' – in fact, anything that smacks of excellence. I don't subscribe to that philosophy; and anyone who is brought up on it will find life a trial because it is full of challenges, whether we want them or not. Resilience is a critical life-skill; to deny someone access to it is culpable. That is only an opinion: you are welcome to take a different view, but only if you can find a convincing rationale for it.

At the beginning of this chapter we talked about the swagger stick of leadership. In his book about Sandhurst, Major General Paul Nanson describes how some of the earliest lessons for officer cadets are not directly about soldiering, they are about self-presentation:

- Stand up straight.
- Be upstanding and worthy of respect.
- Look others in the eye.
- Shake hands firmly.
- The right posture helps you to recalibrate yourself.
- Back yourself.
- Be smart in appearance, and tidy in habit.
- Lose the invisible limits you have imposed on yourself.

He could have added: carry a virtual swagger stick. As professionals we should act and move with pride based not on hubris but on self-confidence and self-knowledge. Good leaders carry the aura of quality around with them.

5

THE LEADER AS A TEAM PLAYER

Bonding, valuing, and listening to the band

TEAMS   TEAM PLAYERS   RESPECT   ALLOWABLE WEAKNESS

As a small child, I remember Sunday afternoon concerts in the park by military bands (a few such concerts still exist, though now the musicians are usually civilians, albeit in uniform). Nowadays, we see military bands mostly on television on ceremonial occasions. But have you ever stopped to wonder why the military spend time, money, and personnel on making music? There are good reasons, and we'll return to them, and their significance for educational leaders, at the end of the chapter.

★★★

Most leaders begin their serious leadership journey by role modelling; appreciating and copying someone else's style. I did exactly that. I had been a teacher, a head of department, a teacher trainer, and the head of a service unit for fellow trainers. People obviously judged that I did the various roles effectively, including the leadership ones, because my career was progressing, but I was giving the process of leadership insufficient thought. Then I was appointed the co-ordinator of a Government project on teacher education. Suddenly I was looking after day-to-day budget management, carrying out research and recruiting other research teams, appointing research assistants, working with the university campuses, gathering authors from all over the country, dealing with publishers, and heading off for days at a time to disseminate outcomes from the project. Luckily, my line manager at the time, a young professor called Ted Wragg, was a role model manager. He had the experience to guide research, the intellect to think through strategy, the tools to write in various styles, a healthy attitude to audiences, to a large extent the personal skills to keep everyone interested, and a pleasant manner in dealing with staff, support personnel, and the government civil servants who put up the money! The penny quickly dropped that the project's activities were very significant in the climate of the time, but that the significance could be lost unless the project itself and its outcomes (for clients, customers, fellow educators whom we were trying to influence) were led effectively. To do that a lot people had to work, often in isolated pockets, but towards a common vision. We needed teamwork, and leadership was about keeping the teams 'on song' and motivated. Suddenly, one became aware of the power of leadership in progressing others towards goals, in increasing the effectiveness of the individual through collaboration, and in changing the context in which one operated. As a leader I grew overnight in both understanding and performance skills.

Coincidentally at that time, there was a lot of research going on to discover what makes a good leader. It has been going on ever since, and no one has come up with a definitive answer, though many contributory factors have been identified and will be discussed in this chapter. I warn the reader now: there will be blueprints but not moulds. What makes an effective leader? If we knew the answers we wouldn't need to ask the question.

★★★

How do we know if we are team players? What follows is a real example, though the names have been changed.

I started a new job in which I was responsible for the in-service education of more than 5,000 teachers. There were issues to be dealt with in the first months, and my predecessor had been asked to stay on for some weeks to induct me into the very wide geographical area the job covered. As it happened, he had already arranged to host a conference during that time; it was his conference not mine, so I just went along as an observer. The first exercise was meant to be a bonding activity, carried out in pairs, to help us to get to know one another and learn to work together for the next two days. My buddy was Jack, a high-flying Chief Education Officer of almost god-like status. The details of the task are vague now, but it involved trading information with other pairs. We were supposed to tell the truth, and there would be a winner. We had two minutes in our pairs to get to know one another before the task began. I said to Jack: 'I hate these games'. Jack said to me: 'So do I; do you want to win?' I affirmed that otherwise it was a waste of time playing. We agreed we would lie through our teeth and win the game. We were frighteningly convincing. We won. Then one of the delegates asked: 'Was everything you said true?' We laughed and said none of it was true. We were sent to Coventry by the other delegates, who had wanted to win but failed to realise that you couldn't tell the truth and win.

So were Jack and I team players? Well, all the other delegate pairs had tried to be – to follow the rules and win the game by collaboration with each other and with the other pairs. But the reason Jack and I won the game was because we had the strongest bond and backed each other up totally and unflinchingly. We played for ourselves *and* each other. The others *thought* they were good team players. We *knew* we were. They complained that, had they lied, they might have won. But Jack put it bluntly: 'You didn't suss out the game. You didn't lie. You didn't win'. You can decide for yourself. Maybe we should look at some examples and definitions of team working to help your decision.

★★★

What most of us understand by a team in an educational context is a collection of teaching staff and (optionally) administrators at various levels in the institution who come together to lead and co-ordinate actions that have the intention of improving the running, practice, or outcomes of the educational processes in or across that institution. Teams will have leaders; they usually play the dual role of member and leader, though a leader could be more or less hands-on. In specific circumstances other personnel connected with the institution might join the team (governors, pupils, parents).

One kind of team activity which often works extremely well is team teaching. A model which indicates the basic characteristics might look like this:

> Three teachers who between them are form tutors for all the classes in a year group decide that they would like to work more closely together to deliver the curriculum. They have access to rooms which can be joined by operating folding screens. They co-plan their work and play to one another's strengths. One might take all the students for science and mathematics lessons;

another assumes responsibility for history, geography, RE, and social lessons; the third picks up on the expressive arts. One or two specialists provide specific lessons like PE while the team members teach the specialists' students. The year group is served by two support staff, and they make occasional inputs in areas where they have specific knowledge. Sometimes all the staff are present at once, but sometimes a team member will be released in order to carry out planning, preparation of learning materials, or administration work such as booking an out-of-school visit. The students gain by having a variety of expertise, more specialist-led lessons, and a variety of teaching styles and voices. The staff keep their personal tutor groups but gain a wider knowledge of the year group as a whole. All the members of the team take a lead role in their areas of expertise; but one of them acts as convenor and co-ordinator for the work overall.

One young teacher who moved from conventional class teaching to working in a teaching team reflected on her experience:

> Being part of the team has been a liberating experience. I feel constantly supported by having more experienced people around me; but that doesn't mean they stifle my initiatives. I was actually very surprised that they were happy to stand back and let me lead, and especially to contribute things where I felt that I had really good knowledge… But it isn't only the content. I can watch them actually teaching and how they deal with situations that arise in the lesson – and that helps me reflect on my teaching skills. I've become very friendly with all the team members and it's really helped to induct me into the profession. M, the team leader, expects me to pull my weight, but boosts what I do in front of the children and gives me pointers when we are away from them.

All teamwork, whatever the team's task, involves followers and leaders, and sometimes an individual will play one role and sometimes the other. So what are the putative advantages of working in teams?

★★★

Not everyone is temperamentally disposed to work primarily in teams, but those who do make a number of claims for the experience. As in the quotation above, there is often an increased sense of involvement, which helps to promote a feeling of ownership in the enterprise. You could also feel in the quotation a sense of security which may, in turn, make it easier to try new things and take risks. Motivation and morale are raised by the experience, especially given a decreased fear of failure. The feeling of 'being in it together' is important, too: shared goals, shared information, shared understandings about the intentions for the activity. Ideas and people are mutually valued.

Some might read the quotation and dismiss it as relevant only to a primary school setting, but that would be a total misunderstanding. I have been active in the same kind of system as a secondary teacher, and even in university settings. Teams are a way of working; age-related issues are simply irrelevant.

Teams also have potentials which were not hinted at above. More people delivering the curriculum in this way may increase expertise for the students – they experience not just a range of subject knowledge, but all the interests and experiences of the teaching team can be utilised. This has the potential to increase the creativity of the work, which will be informed by a wider range of ideas, leading to fuller and more satisfying understandings and outcomes.

Managerially, teams have advantages, too. Pooled abilities and experiences of the team members may help resolve issues of how to present material or manage the student group. Team decisions are more satisfying than those made in isolation. As team members learn how each thinks and acts, their work will become more intuitive and time-saving. Leading the team should provide a sense of satisfaction, but it also removes the isolation experienced by many beginning leaders.

To work effectively, team members do not have to be of an age (it's often better if they are not); they do not have to hang out together after work (though some do); the members may be introverts or extraverts; ideally, differences are as important as similarities in belief, approach, and methods of working. There is a fallacy that people must like one another to perform effectively as a team: this is not true. In a book about civil airline accidents, one expert on dealing with critical situations recommends that an aircraft captain can encourage crew members to be assertive at the same time as maintaining command.

There is one characteristic of teams which cannot be substituted by the lone worker: that collected wisdom is more important than individual ability. This is a mantra that I have followed in my career. Throughout much of my research – for the government during the Teacher Education Project, for the Schools' Council in its research into Topic Work, during my work on school organisation with the Funding Agency for Schools – the intention has been, consistently, to bring the best of many professionals' insights together[1]. One problem from which academics suffer is their reluctance to expose their great idea/s; they don't want them to be copied or appropriated, so they become what Freud labelled anally retentive. But professional wisdom is only active and useful if it is shared. The language of many academic texts is often so dense as to be almost unintelligible. An idea, however brilliant, which is not communicated effectively, is a sterile idea. As academics we all learn to write what I have sometimes called 'intellectual clap-trap' – we must in order to get the next job! But the work that has given me the greatest pleasure has been the ideas which I have shared with fellow professionals, and they with me, in plain language. Obscurity can often be a cover for ignorance.

★★★

To date in this chapter I have made the case for teams, a case built on the widely expressed beliefs of the teaching profession, and have relayed some of my own experience of team working and team leading – which can undoubtedly be both pleasurable and effective. But…

There is always a 'But…'. As I sat pondering what I had written, a phrase dropped into my mind: one of those annoying little phrases that comes like a temptation from some little devil in a C.S. Lewis novel. The phrase was: 'a bit romanticised'. I confess, I had never read or heard anyone use that phrase about teams, and the phrase worried me because I knew that in some corner of my intellect I must have a doubt about the received wisdom of team working. So, since the devil had struck and the devil makes work, my idle hands played with the phrase on my keyboard, and up popped these thoughts from a respected American called James Meindl:

- People have gone overboard with the notion of teams.
- Teams and teamwork don't stand up to the scrutiny of science.
- Research has not provided very much evidence regarding the superior effectiveness of teams. Yet teams are a favoured method of getting things done.

- The popularity of teamwork outweighs the evidence.

Don't you just hate little devils! (Though, as an aside, if you are looking to write one, Meindl's propositions would be a great topic for a PhD thesis.)

So now I have exposed a potential weakness in my own argument, you will want me to explain why I think it has come about. The answer lies in the soil from which teamwork sprouted: it was not education but business. Business and education are not the same animal. That is not to say that education has nothing to learn from business; it may well have much to learn. But it is not the poor relation of business. Business is not its guru, mentor, and intellectual superior. So education must milk business ideas and concepts for what they are worth, but not get hung up on thinking itself inferior. The strengths of team working, as delineated above, are real and valuable. But teamwork is only one possible genre of educational activity and needs to be translated to its own context and appraised against that.

So here are four claims that are made for team working in educational settings; and you must use your experiences and insights to test them:

- The team gives the leader, team members, and students access to a wider talent-pool than would otherwise be the case.
- This involves exposure to a wider range of perspectives, knowledge, and opinions.
- Members communicate more, collaborate better, and share goals and intentions.
- Collaborative working has advantages for the leader and the team members, and their job satisfaction: they develop better interpersonal relations and have more fun (important in these days of sensitivity to mental health issues).

★★★

Back in the early 1990s I had the great pleasure to meet with the late Meredith Belbin,[2] who provided, at the time (and whose work still is, in my view), the most insightful examination of team working. Belbin had investigated the roles a team needed to make it effective and which a leader should seek out in constructing a team. There were nine key roles, but for the sake of easy reading I have listed them in Table 5.1 on the following page, along with a brief definition of each one. In

Table 5.1 Belbin's team roles

Resource investigator	Good at generating ideas and finding solutions.
Team worker	The person who helps the members to gel and collaborate.
Co-ordinator	Keeps everyone focused and delegates tasks appropriately.
Plant	Is a creative and problem-solver but may be hard to live with.
Monitor-evaluator	Logical and level-headed, weighs up options and their respective values.
Specialist	May not be a regular team member, but provides vital skills and information.
Shaper	Is the driver and enthusiast who challenges others.
Implementer	Is good at devising workable strategies for the team.
Completer-finisher	The person who looks at the small print and dots the 'i's of the outcome.
NB One person can play more than one role; any player may have allowable weaknesses.	

Belbin's view, all the roles needed to be covered within a team, but smaller teams could double-up the roles as necessary. What I particularly liked was that Belbin did not shirk the hard questions about the 'awkward' people who don't, on the face of it, seem to be team players. To deal with the problem, two of his notions seemed particularly apt. First, he accepted that a team may not contain within itself all the expertise to deal with their chosen project. To this end, the team could expand itself by engaging in conversation with an Expert. That simple proposition deals with the difficulty of lack of knowledge. The other notion was applicable to all roles and dealt with something more akin to a personality issue – and Belbin called it 'allowable weakness'.

Allowable weakness is tinged with absolute realism. For example, in a team there may well be an individual who sees the glass as half empty, always cautions against haste, wants to dot every 'i', or won't invest to accumulate because risk is anathema. These individuals may signal lack of interest – they may turn up late to meetings, forget to bring documents, or lack apparent concentration. Though they may seem not to be pulling with the team, their contributions may actually be entirely reasonable and valuable. They may help balance uncritical enthusiasm. Give me allowable weaknesses over blind optimism or conformity every time.

One of the most moving letters I ever received from a team member on leaving my post came from someone who was widely regarded as the kill-joy. Bill was a talented man – literate, inventive, quirky, humorous, and deeply insightful – but a sceptic through and through. I took to him instantly and was delighted to have him a member of the team. On my resignation he wrote:

> Thank you for all your patience during our time served together. I can honestly say that, over many years within this employment, it has been the first time that anyone was prepared to listen to me, to consider my arguments, to look at my point of view. I haven't always agreed with the decisions of the team, but I knew that at least someone had considered what I had to say.

I found that deeply moving. Moral: a leader 'listens' – not as politicians listen who hear and do their own thing – but as one who weighs the objection and is prepared to re-group.

★★★

To date, then, we have looked at the alleged pros and cons of team working and team leading, but there are other issues that insinuate themselves into our consciousness. These issues need to be addressed and I propose to do this through a set of brief questions and answers. (You are not obliged to accept my answers, of course; you can consult the literature, your colleagues or your own experience to make a judgement).

> What, then, can we conclude about the relative merits of team working and autonomous action by the leader?

Teams work and can be shown to work, but that doesn't mean that working in teams should be an exclusive model, nor that team working is best for every situation. Teaching teams work when the participants enjoy that way of working and the physical conditions exist to accommodate it; but some teachers hate it, and some do it but do it badly. Having management teams across an institution (let's say, for finance, for infrastructure, for social care, for academic results) may be helpful, but ultimately the whole picture needs to come together for the institution to function seamlessly. Later, in Chapter 10, we discuss the charismatic leader syndrome. It too can work in the right circumstances, given the right person, the right conditions, the right context.

Are there gender issues that affect team working?

To date, this is an under-researched area of teams in education contexts. Whether men or women are more likely to favour team working is not clear. Nor is it clear whether gender balances alter the ways teams work or their ethos. No doubt there will be a lot more investigation into these questions, so let's just conclude the jury is currently out.

Does team working make for rivalry between groups of staff?

If there are a number of teams doing parallel tasks, then the answer is 'maybe'. For example, if each department or year group is challenged to improve its results, then some teams may push to out-perform others. The upside of this may be improved student outcomes in some areas of work; the downside may be heightened stress on students and staff. Life is not so much a cabaret as a set of scales, no action is either value-free or without (unforeseen) consequence.

Is team working an effective form of delegation?

Some senior managers seem to treat it as such. Delegation might mean that a head teacher turns tasks over to appropriate people within their leadership team. Delegation can help with team collaboration and development as well as overall productivity. Delegating the right tasks to the right people can increase overall productivity. However, delegation may be seen as imposition by the delegate.

Are some people more, or less, capable by virtue of personality of being team players?

Teams can be made up of very disparate individuals. Let's take a fictional example with one of the most popular televised teams of all – the A-Team. Lieutenant Colonel 'Hannibal' Smith the hard-man team-leader, suave but a strategist; Lieutenant Templeton 'Faceman' Peck provided a bit of glamour and the ability to act a part; Sergeant 'Bad Attitude' Baracus was the aeroplane-hating grumpy one with the allowable weaknesses; and Captain 'Howlin' Mad' Murdock was the inventive, quirky, intellectual with a tendency to behave abnormally. They were all misfits but they melded, complemented one another's skills, shared a cause – and they usually won through and rejoiced when their plans came together.

Teamwork is about bonding and about valuing one another and one another's skills. The leader's great skill is to help all members of the team, whatever its purpose, to do these two things. So that just leaves the Band which I promised, in the introduction to the chapter, that I would re-visit.

★★★

How are military bands relevant to the concept of education leadership?

Army musicians probably have their origins in earliest times and primarily for the purpose of communication: a human voice would not carry over the sound of battle while a drum or a trumpet was more efficient. Music also helps to beat out the rhythm of marching (ensures progress) and lifts the spirits (heightens morale). Increasingly, at big public events such as the annual Trooping the Colour ceremony extremely large bands must manoeuvre on a parade ground where space is restricted. To do this, a relatively modern formation has been invented: the spin wheel. How this works is something of a dark art even to those involved. The spectators hear the music, see the spinning wheel of musicians, watch the senior bandsmen guide the formation, tremble when the band splits and faces in opposite directions, but is enthralled at the perfect finale.

This description encapsulates perfectly the multidirectional movement, confusion, apparent errors, and final triumph of an educational institution being led effectively (compare the video version of the spin wheel on the web[3]). The director of music keeps the music flowing and everyone in tune; the drum majors and bandmasters (senior leaders) control their individual segments of the formation; the senior NCOs enveloped in the ranks (the other experienced leaders at various levels) hold their nerve and ensure everyone else is in the right place; and the troops (staff, students) work under pressure to produce an impressive performance.

Leadership, in teams or out of them, at every level of seniority, is about staying in tune, keeping in synch, and delivering the intentions.

6

SETTING AN EXAMPLE – HAVING A VISION AND LEADING FROM THE FRONT

Developing the courage to lead

COURAGE INDEPENDENCE LEADING FROM THE FRONT & BEHIND

I was unwell for a few weeks recently. A friend sent me a book by Ichiro Kishimi and Fumitake Koga called *The Courage to be Disliked* (you might think that is an unlikely title to send even to a short-term invalid, but my friend is a quirky kind of guy who was a member of one of my teams). It transpired that the book was mostly an exposition of Adlerian psychology, and it does have a relevance to leadership.

Alfred Adler was born in 1870 and died in 1937; he had worked with Freud but departed from Freud's views and branched out into theories of his own. Two related ideas of Adler's will suffice as an introduction to his influence. First, Adler felt that we are not shaped by events, but that we can shape them to control our own destinies; indeed we can decide as early as childhood what (in general terms) our ambitions are and can begin to shape ourselves towards them even if they are later modified: we are not the victims of 'drives' but actively change situations by our responses to them. Second, our lives are shaped by our own dynamic striving when faced with emergent situations: we are goal-directed and *we* choose the goals. So Adler puts a good deal of emphasis on self-determination in our overall life-approach.

Readers of a certain generation will have cottoned on by now that this Adler (Alfred) is not to be confused with that other, more famous, Adler (Larry) who played a mean harmonica. But there is a serendipitous connection. Larry chose his goal of harmonica playing as a child, strove to be the best, played every genre of music from classical to pop, had massive career setbacks at the beginning, overcame the setbacks to achieve his goals, and became world-famous and an innovator – a classic Alfred Adlerian life. He had self-belief and courage. In fact, in his later life, Larry was so well known to impresarios and potentates that his friends joked and said his personal anthem should be 'Name Drops Keep Falling On My Head'.

Often, the outcome of strong self-determination is that it offends some of the people around us. The determined character is spoken of as 'getting on', 'bettering themselves', of 'getting out of our league' and many other such phrases. Inevitably, this gradual alienation will be construed by the onlookers as the person 'getting above him/herself' and that the onlookers are no longer 'good enough' for the aspirant. Much of this reaction may be perception rather than truth, but perceptions often produce their own 'truths'. So an aspirant leader, as someone with a goal who makes choices to achieve that goal, may well become disliked – and we're back to the title of that Kishimi and Koga book, and the notion of courage.

This chapter, then, will have two major themes:

- Don't become a leader under the false impression that you will become a sociological star and everyone will love and revere you.
- If you can't take the criticism, the flak, and rejections of leadership, you might be better off not to start down the road.

If you do start down the road, remember and take comfort: after winning the Second World War, Winston Churchill was voted out of office.

★★★

Courage. The word has been used already several times in this chapter. In the education settings which our leaders occupy, what exactly does it mean? What are its dimensions?

In popular thought, courage may be defined into six types:

- Physical
- Social

- Moral
- Emotional
- Intellectual
- Spiritual.

We need to turn first to physical courage and clear some ground about this emotive topic. Physical courage is rarely called upon in educational settings; but I did say 'rarely' not 'never'. In April 2019 the BBC reported that nearly a quarter of teachers say they face violence (i.e. from students) on a weekly basis. The suggestion raises a lot of questions (in my view) about the representativeness of the sample of teachers involved, and the ways in which the data were gathered. If that experience were genuinely representative and repeated uniformly across the entire teaching profession nationwide, it would be a staggering statistic. One problem is that the media do like to hype up these situations, and they probably do more harm than good by so doing. This came home to me very forcibly when a colleague told me of something that happened to him as a very young teacher working in an urban secondary school:

> I was aware that my class of 40 students were very restive and were passing messages under the desks. I couldn't work out what the issue was, and eventually I said to them: 'Look, I know something's going on. Let's get the problem out in the open'. One student asked me: 'Do you know who Mr X is?' I said I did; he was my opposite number in the school down the road. The student proffered a local newspaper, folded to reveal a lurid double-page spread: 'Teacher beaten up by his students', it read; 'He will be off work for six months'. Another student sneered: 'What would happen if we decided to beat you up? There's a lot of us!'

This is the kind of moment when you might have to stop and think – but preferably not for many microseconds. He made a spur-of-the-moment joke of the threat (good move – humour is a positive force in difficult times), gave the students a fleeting moment to reflect, and then suggested: 'Aren't you bored with this rubbish? I know you wouldn't do that, so let's not waste any more time on it. Shall we pick up from where we left off last lesson…?'

They didn't beat him up. They probably (no — certainly) never wanted to. They weren't angels, but they definitely weren't thugs. They were provoked by irresponsible reporting.

So, teachers can't rule out the need for physical courage. Youngsters are like animals, they smell fear. I used to tell my trainee teachers who asked about physical threats: you are allowed to be afraid, but don't sweat or shake. But the threat (where there is one) relates to teachers overall, your team, not to leaders specifically — and it might be worth considering whether a good education leader can do anything to mitigate the problem. (Before I do this, I am going to step aside and ask you a question that will not be universally popular. If you started from a blank canvas and invented a system that would gainfully occupy young people from three to 18 years old, would you devise one that kept them confined mainly inside buildings for 40 weeks a year, carrying round a heavy load of books, sitting uncomfortably for four or five hours a day, statically carrying out tasks about whose purpose they often can't see the point, and listening for several hours daily when even an adult's concentration span is reckoned to average about eight seconds?)

What an education leader has on his/her side in this situation is the ability to influence the climate within their area of responsibility: a year leader sets the ethos across a year-group of students; a subject leader controls the ethos of the subject teaching. My experience is that it is possible to control the climate to such an extent that the majority of potential conflict situations never actually materialise. This is an example of that principle in action:

A year leader becomes aware of restive and aggressive behaviour among the student group. He calls the teachers and classes together and talks through the problem. What emerges is not that the students have a specific aggression to their learning, but a deep malaise about their lives and their community. One student sums it up: 'We live in a dump; and we hate it — so we kick against it. Then we get into trouble, so we kick a bit harder'. The year leader suggests that the students spend roughly eight hours a day in school, eight in their community, and eight asleep. He suggests that the eight sleeping hours may not be too bad; and that school has limited control over those spent at home in the community. But the year teachers do have control over the other eight hours each day. If the year staff can provide the most interesting work they can, and try to create a better, more friendly atmosphere than that of the community for that eight hours, then at least some part of each day won't feel so bad. The students agree it's worth a try. The year leader asks them what three or four simple rules would make their school experience better, and the students formulate them:

- Don't push, shove or be aggressive.
- Everyone should speak politely.
- Don't talk over others or shout.
- Behave maturely.

Now the students have ownership of the problem. Staff agree to encourage the principles so that they in turn don't have to get angry or raise their voices. When things get a bit out of control everyone will pull back and examine whether the rules are being kept. The result is a change of tone: incidents of student–student aggression decrease; the students do not behave aggressively or rudely to staff; staff remind offenders about the contract rather than rushing in with sanctions, and if they get a bit cross they say 'sorry'.

A solution like this sounds simple and obvious, but for the leader it takes courage to step outside the authoritarian role of laying down the law, and to hand over some control. Yet from personal experience I know it can work, and often it changes atmospheres. With the change comes a lowering of stress for everyone, and so the tensions reduce on a downward spiral.

Consider this leadership problem:

> With a sudden rise in the incidence of minor bullying, the proposal is put forward to install CCTV cameras on the ends of corridors and the approaches to the toilets in the school. As a head of year, you will lead the debate among your team about their response to this proposal. What factors will you draw to their attention, and how will you aim to reach a consensus to put to the Senior Management Team?

One has to be honest (and be aware) about potential violence in schools; there will always be communities where these things are more frequent but in the vast majority of cases it need not be the issue the Press sometimes makes it out to be. It is more likely that aggression against teachers or heads will come from parents rather than students. As I wrote this chapter the *Mail Online* posted a story (rapidly dropped) about the use of body-cams and fluo jackets by teachers in schools. Three examples were cited, but one was only a school contemplating their use; one was their use to protect school students from non-students; and a single case related to a trial to forestall 'low level disruption' – so a non-story. Another source stated that two other trials in schools had 'fizzled out'. But it reminded me of a day when I insisted that a university dean (not an educationist) come to see the in-service work his staff were doing in a large Academy. After six months' persuasion he came. The principal took him on a walk-about. Four large sixth formers approached down the corridor – and passed us. I was behind the dean and the principal with another staff member. At an opportune moment the dean leaned back and spoke in my ear: 'I feel quite safe here really', he confided. His six months of reticence had been because of a perception he would get mugged on the corridor!

This is a book about leadership, not discipline in schools, but there are a few pointers which school leaders might take on board to some benefit:

- Schools where staff and students trust one another and have informal but respectful personal relations are less likely to have deep anger festering under the surface.
- Schools that set a tone of mature behaviour, interesting work, controlled movement, cheerfulness, humour and calm are likely to reduce everyone's tension.
- If teachers signal that they care about their students – not just grades, but how they think, how they feel, what they are interested in beyond the classroom, their personal difficulties, their aspirations – then relations are much less likely to get strained.
- When a situation does arise, it needs to be dealt with quickly and preferably away from the sight and sound of others who might be tempted to join the debate.
- As a last resort, teachers should always work through their line managers, the head, the police, and their unions.

Students should not view teachers as the enemy, teachers should not treat students as a hostile force. The education leader has a role to play in this. For the education leader, there are other kinds of courage beyond physical courage, and to those we now turn.

★★★

What of those other five dimensions of courageous leadership:

- Social
- Moral
- Emotional
- Intellectual
- Spiritual?

The last of these – spiritual courage – is an intensely personal matter and I don't intend to discuss it here. Those leaders who have a religious faith may find it a refuge when times are hard; they may benefit from being part of a supportive community. For my part, I would never enquire about an individual's faith, nor would I express a view for or against the notion: some things are best left to the person concerned. I would contend, for example, that the prolific author and champion of atheism, Professor Richard Dawkins, has as much of a 'faith' as most Christians have; it is just differently constructed and comes to different conclusions. It needs to be noted that a lot of claims have been made for superior student progress in faith schools; without prejudice, it has to be admitted that researchers find it very hard to untangle 'faith' as a variable from other socio-economic factors which may be present. In Malta, where faith schools are more common, I do believe that some, at least, create an ethos in which (it can be shown that) faith is a positive factor in the education of the 'whole student'.

However, moral courage is a different matter. Moral courage is the ability to behave according to one's principles even when under pressure from peers or superiors to do something different. Moral courage should never become insubordination or mere whim, but does apply when a serious matter of principle is at stake. One debate that occurred when Academy schools were introduced by the government was about funding. Though the start-up incentives were high (the government often put in a lot of money to schools choosing this route), it was clear to anyone with a financial brain that the money would run out and that Academies would need to raise a proportion of their own costs either through sponsorship, or by selling services, or by some other means. Many teachers and leaders in schools were, and are, totally opposed to this notion: education, they claim, should be a right; they are not salespersons nor are they convinced by the ethics of begging or advertising. Schools as businesses was a concept foreign to them.

Academies that raised money successfully flourished. Those that did not struggled. Some teachers moved out of jobs in that sector, but others liked the entrepreneurial feel of the new system. Resentment between staff, however, sometimes occurred, based on the feeling that some who disapproved of fundraising were nonetheless ready to benefit from the cash. Social courage and moral courage may be related in that taking a specific stance on an issue may lead to antagonism or even ostracism by colleagues. Here are just a few examples of situations I have come across where someone took a principled stance, but the question is – were they right or wrong? How should their colleagues have reacted to them?

- Mr Z, a senior colleague and leader, resigned from his post and went on a lower grade to a nearby school because his head teacher had decided to institute a dress-code for staff on grounds of health and safety, to ensure that dress was 'fit for purpose' for specific activities, and to uphold professional standards.
- I discovered a colleague of mine, Jay, was very depressed and on the verge of leaving the school. He was an active young man, and popular with the students, as well as a good teacher. While we ate our lunchtime sandwiches together, I asked him what was wrong. He said he was on the verge of resigning because he had an empty lesson on his timetable and the head had asked him to fill it with a weekly games' session. He had adamantly refused as he hated all sports. The head had dug his heels in. I decided to talk to the head without Jay's knowledge – Mr G was very approachable. The trouble was they had both dug themselves metaphorical pits and could not climb out without losing face. I suggested to Mr G that we all had to take the odd lesson we were not really qualified for but, if he wished, he could say I had volunteered for the games' session; in return, he might ask Jay to take an English literature lesson from my timetable as a gesture of good will. They both jumped at the chance to relieve themselves of a situation which was, in itself, trivial but had got out of hand.

- Influential members of staff in a primary school believe that they should control the diet of their students because a healthy diet is desirable for young people. They raid the students' lunch boxes and remove what (to them) are offending items. The action raises a number of questions: about the rights and responsibilities of teachers, students, and parents; about discrimination, given the varied social status of the parents across the school and their respective incomes; about the effect these actions might have on students' self-perceptions, and so on.
- Jason is a member of the school football team. The team coach decides that everyone in the team should wear rainbow laces in their boots. Jason is uncomfortable with this, he wishes to decline. What are you going to say to Jason, the team coach, the team? How will you handle this situation in order to resolve the matter both fairly and ethically?

Emotional courage is a different animal. It is about the mental strength we can bring to the range of personal emotions we feel and those we encounter. We have to deal with our own successes and failures, but also other people's problems. Quite often a leader will have to shoulder the burden of a staff member who is going through bad times. Nothing can erase the impact of a young colleague's spouse dying unexpectedly or of a student who loses a parent in an accident. A harrowing event was when a student blew himself up on a home-made firework – he was appallingly scarred. But there may be other, less worthy, causes that demand the leader's attention. A colleague, Miss Y, noticed that one of her team – an older lady – was always carrying a bottle of water around (nothing too odd about that), but that she was very dependent on it. Fearing a major health problem, the leader took the lady aside and asked her about it. The teacher made light of it, but Miss Y noticed that the texture of the water in the bottle was unusual. It transpired the 'water' was actually laced with vodka, and the older colleague was in need of some considerable medical and counselling help.

In today's world, the hardest kind of courage to sustain, arguably, is intellectual courage. In a Society which is increasingly litigious, probed by minorities, and swayed by vocal pressure groups, it remains especially hard to cling to one's reasoned and evidenced beliefs. This is not because the evidenced beliefs are questionable, but because social pressure demands that they adopt these, quite other, views. It is (in my opinion) incumbent on every teacher to be the kind of person who questions every statement, investigates the evidence for it, does not then take a fixed and immutable view (evidence can change over time and with new discoveries), and inculcates into students an inquiring approach rather than one built on prejudice, preference, and partiality.

At a time when even universities (the ultimate aspiration of many of our school students) are being bullied into limiting freedom of speech and debate – even into rewriting history – by those who espouse specific causes, it is tragic to imagine that our once great, open, and internationally valued intellectual institutions are being sacrificed on the altar of pressure groups. Education leaders of the next decades will need the moral courage (integrity) to stand up for the true nature of education. If they don't, then future generations of students will not turn into the enquiring, discerning, and mature individuals we have come to expect; they will be the victims of a system that ends in indoctrination of the kind found in totalitarian régimes. This presents serious dilemmas for leaders in schools:

How do you, and the people you lead, maintain in your lessons a balance between freedom of thought and speech, the expression of minority views, the ability to understand that each generation sees the world with its own perspective, the importance of evidence, the critical approach to statistics and/or information sources (newspapers, TV and e-journalism, the interpretation of images), etc.? What can you do to raise students' (and, if necessary, staff) awareness of issues like propaganda, public hysteria, acting on impulse but without consideration, and discerning bias?

Leadership requires of its holders courage that is multifaceted, exacting, and exhausting. What makes it worth doing is its intrinsic value to ourselves and to future generations.

★★★

A leader stands out from the crowd, but he or she does so by leading a team. This last segment of the chapter listens to the wisdom of people who have been leaders and done the leadership thing successfully in a range of fields: collected wisdom is always more desirable than individual wisdom. Chris Hadfield, astronaut, and former Commander of the International Space Station, saw the significance of this. He pointed out that leadership is not about glorious acts but about keeping the team motivated and focused on a goal; the leader maps the ground and then encourages others to shine.

Leading from the front sometimes involves leading from behind, though it takes just as much courage and a lot of trust. Anita Roddick, founder of The Body Shop, captured the tone of this approach when she tried to model employees who personified what she wanted from her organisation.

We have to be 'in it together' as leaders; a 'band of brothers' united in the common cause of education (or at least, our bit of it). When things get tough, we have to protect the weakest, to have our *Saving Private Ryan* moments. As a leader, you have to be tougher on yourself than on other people.

Leaders may be confident, reasoned, and driven by conviction, but they are never arrogant. Leaders are respectful and they care. If you want to know what people are really like, take a look at how they treat others.

The stage on which our leadership is played out may not be so dramatic, but the warning of Colonel Tim Collins, in a masterful speech before his troops went into battle in Iraq[1], still hangs over us: 'You will be shunned unless your conduct is of the highest – for your deeds will follow you down through history'.

But the awesomeness of being an education leader is summed up in the simple but deeply meaningful sentiments expressed by Nelson Mandela and others in various phrases that make the same point: education is a powerful weapon; it can change the world.

★★★

We've talked about courage, but where does this courage come from?

It can only come from within you, arising out of your integrity, your convictions, your knowledge, your skills, and your commitment.

7

THE IMPORTANCE OF PLANNING
The cautionary tale of the Typhoon jet

VISION   PLANNING   SMEALCS

Major projects frequently fail to go to plan. Take the Typhoon aircraft (the one that currently chases Russian intruders out of the North Sea). In 1988, Parliament was informed its cost would be £7 billion. But that soon almost doubled to some £13 billion, and by 1997 had increased to around £17 billion. The aircraft were due to be in service in 2003 but the cost was escalated to £20 billion and the project was 54 months late. The National Audit Office in 2011 thought the eventual programme cost would hit £37 billion.

In public life, this story is repeated constantly: for example, new road developments, HS2. In 2017, 70 per cent of the 143 major government projects then current had a red or amber warning for over-running cost. But the same initial optimism often afflicts even small-scale undertakings in industry, commerce, the NHS, and education around the country. The commonest mis-judgements are that things will happen quicker, cost less, and be more effective than the reality.

Effective planning may be part of the solution. Part of the solution might also be intelligent guesswork (but we will return to that later), and no plan can be viable until the planner has a vision (*quo vide*). Clearly, however, the planning process is important, and it is critical for leaders to master it.

In my role as a tutor of leadership skills, and even more importantly as a leader at various levels in the education service, I have often been called on to talk about what constitutes effective planning. The literature of educational leadership is replete with systems and schemes – more or less practical, more or less theoretical, more or less researched, more or less fanciful. In the end, though, planning is a pretty simple process even when the plan's context is wide-ranging and complex. In fact, simplicity is a virtue; it makes the plan more manageable, and more likely to be understood and to succeed.

You would be right to challenge me at this point: 'Come on then, tell us the simple secret of how to plan effectively'. I will, but first a paragraph of anecdotal context.

When I was 14 the secondary school I attended had a Combined Cadet Force and everyone was required to join one of the service arms. I signed the Official Secrets Act and became an infantry cadet in the King's Royal Rifles. It was great. I enjoyed the uniform, the 'bull' (yes, honestly), the marching, having a real rifle with real bullets to shoot at outdoor targets, snap shooting on the indoor range, sewing on the chevrons, and so on. But there was also some more cerebral stuff. As an NCO you ran a section of 11 other cadets; and you had to carry out 'missions' involving crossing open ground and streams, using cover, camouflage, and achieving combat objectives. To do this there was an acronym that has come to play a part in the whole of my leadership life: SMEALCS.

SMEALCS stood for situation, mission, execution, administration, logistics, command, signals. I am going to translate this notion for you in terms of educational leadership and relate it to three generic problems.

> Note: As stated, in the following portion of the chapter I am going to apply SMEALCS as a planning tool to three education problems: Scenario 1, A failing curriculum unit; Scenario 2, Use of school plant; Scenario 3, Use of human resources. You can read the section up to the next asterisk straight through in its entirety as printed, following all three scenarios under each SMEALCS heading. Or, if you prefer, you can read the section up to the next asterisk three times, following one scenario at a time – you choose which works best for you. For those who find the acronym SMEALCS a problem, I have substituted a question alongside each heading – though it militates against the easy memorisation of the system.

SITUATION – WHERE ARE WE NOW?

To progress to anywhere, you must begin from somewhere – your current location. In an educational context we are at Point A. Point A is the problem we need to solve and the location from which we need to move on. Without a clear appraisal of that, no movement is likely to be in a positive direction.

In the examples quoted, the problem(s) to be solved is/are:

Scenario 1, Curriculum. Our segment of curriculum is not well delivered by staff, boring for students, and results in depressed performance in examinations. We need to understand why these factors occur – so a bit of analysis is flagged up here. A good leader will explore the issues with students and staff, building a picture of weaknesses (but also any strengths that might be preserved).

Scenario 2, School plant. The school plant is scattered, and students are losing time moving about between teaching sessions. We need to know what time is being lost, what alternative models might exist, and the level of improved time-usage that might be achieved.

Scenario 3, Human resource. A department is currently timetabled so that learning sessions are all covered by qualified teachers, but the styles of teaching in use don't seem to mesh with the preferred learning styles of the pupils. The leader needs assess how teacher strengths, interest, and talent can be more effectively integrated with the needs and interests of the individual student groups.

MISSION – WHERE DO WE WANT TO BE?

That is, where do we want to arrive at the end of this process, in a year's time, or on some other identified timescale? Mission is Point B: the goal towards which we are attempting to move. This goal needs to be delineated as precisely as possible. It may have more than one element; but all the intentions should be clearly articulated. For our respective examples the process might go something like this:

Scenario 1, Curriculum. A new, more dynamic curriculum segment needs to be devised and trialled. It has to fit any externally required criteria such as those of Examinations Boards. Content must be engaging to students, and interesting for staff to deliver. Over time, results need to improve. A monitoring system needs to be in place to ensure that these criteria have all been met.

Scenario 2, School plant. The outcome of improving movement around the school plant must result in learning-time gains, but any changes must be feasible. Movement options need to be compared. Staff will want to assess both the resulting learning gains and the practicality of a new movement system for them, for students and for anyone else affected.

Scenario 3, Human resource. The leader needs to explore and identify the mismatches of interest among the staff, and the learning preferences of the student groups. Then timetable changes need to be devised and implemented against agreed monitoring criteria.

EXECUTION – HOW ARE WE GOING TO GET THERE?

Simply: how are we going to achieve the intentions? How are we going to move from Point A to Point B? What are the steps the leader and other colleagues need to take to make the move? Useful aids in the thinking process at this point might be charts, lists, exploded diagrams, or even mind-maps. In the examples, the process might go like this:

Scenario 1, Curriculum. The leader will set up a small, maybe two-person, project team to devise a new segment of curriculum for the team to consider. This might be used experimentally by the team and then tweaked appropriately. Results will then need to be monitored periodically or over a given timescale.

Scenario 2, School plant. Physical checks may need to be made to assess the time taken by students moving round the site, and how much potential learning time is lost. The leader will ask the team to brainstorm alternatives for movement around the site in the light of the outcomes of these measurements. When a preferred option is identified, it may be implemented for a trial period.

Scenario 3, Human resource. A series of class discussions between the leader and the students may help to clarify the problems; the leader will hold informal talks with staff. In the light of these investigations, the leader will implement some timetable changes and put in hand a monitoring process to establish the levels of satisfaction of the students and staff with the new system.

ADMINISTRATION – WHO ARE THE PERSONNEL RESPONSIBLE?

Who are the people who will see through the overall execution of the mission and the sub-sections of it? In the examples:

Scenario 1, Curriculum. The two-person project team will rewrite the curriculum unit. The team will debate it and then trial it. The leader will consider the level by which learning outcomes improve.

Scenario 2, School plant. Following trials, the leader will authorise a change of procedure. A team member may be delegated to explore staff and student satisfaction with the new system. All staff will be asked to assess whether learning outcomes have improved.

Scenario 3, Human resource. The leader will deal with time-table changes and subsequently monitor staff and student satisfaction levels.

Within each of the above scenarios under this heading there are identifiable phases led by individuals – each of these will be allotted an appropriate timescale against which the member/s of staff will deliver their contributions to the changes.

LOGISTICS – WHAT FRESH PERSONNEL, MATERIEL, OR SYSTEM CHANGES DO WE NEED?

What do we need to facilitate the progress from Point A to Point B in each case? For example:

Scenario 1, Curriculum. In the case of revised curriculum, the leader might be able to arrange for the project team to be freed up to be able to work collaboratively on the curriculum unit. They may need new texts or software in order to deliver the revised curriculum.

Scenario 2, School plant. The leader may need to undertake consultations with a wider group of school staff and senior management to see whether proposed changes affect them adversely.

Scenario 3, Human resource. The leader may have to negotiate some knock-on effects of the timetable adjustments with the senior manager responsible.

COMMAND – WHO IS RESPONSIBLE?

Scenarios 1, 2, 3. In each of our cases, the leader is the person responsible for the overall success of the movement from Point A to Point B. Other members of staff, such as the project team in Scenario 1, have identified responsibilities.

SIGNALS – HOW DO WE COMMUNICATE ON THE JOURNEY?

The leader and team members need to mark out and talk to one another about the stages on the journey to achieving the mission, about progress, changes of direction, or final success.

Scenarios 1, 2, 3. In each case, the leader will establish way-mark meetings of the team in line with the deadlines for progress set to its members: these meetings will plot the next steps, including the final deadline for the activity. Appropriate consultation will be undertaken with relevant others outside the team to ensure proposed solutions do not cause problems to other staff. When transition from Point A to Point B is complete: Mission accomplished!

★★★

To summarise SMEALCS, it is an easily remembered, simple system capable of almost infinite adaptation to fit a variety of circumstances, especially if you recall it using the acronym. It can be made more complicated by adding levels of detail, or it can be applied to a very big project because each sub-section of that overall intention can also be planned in turn using exactly the same methodology. It covers all the key bases, but if it doesn't fit a specific situation you can simply add your own additional operations. It's a 'get out of jail' card for every manager, and has a neat internal logic, with each succeeding section building on those that come before.

However, even SMEALCS requires a leader to make some judgements in construing both Point A and the route to Point B. Thus, at the beginning of this chapter, I talked about intelligent guesswork. None of us can unerringly predict the future. So inevitably the leader must make informed (intelligent) judgements (guesses) about how things might move on during, or by the end of, the project, whatever that is. All planning requires realism, and throughout the planning process there will continue to be risks that not everything will go according to plan. An example will suffice:

The curriculum revision Scenario 1 above seems logical and progressive: the path from failing unit to more exciting material leading to improved student outcomes is desirable. The ploy of putting a two-person team in charge of the actual rewriting is a good one if we are let into the secret that the failing unit is favoured as THE way forward by the very traditional longest-serving staff member in the group, and that the two-person team is composed of younger, fresher minds who understand the power of e-learning in the perceptions of students. What we did not know, however, and neither did the leader, is that halfway through the rewriting project one of the two-person project team would make a sudden decision to emigrate without serving out her notice. The leader's plan was a good one, but it is now in jeopardy because of an intelligent (but erroneous) guess that the writing pair would remain together to the end of the project. The leader now has dilemmas to face and options to consider:

- Abandon the project.
- Substitute the missing colleague (but with whom?).
- Put herself in place of the missing colleague.
- Put off further action until someone new (and hopefully suitable) is appointed to the department – and so on.

There is no progress without risk, and even the best laid plans 'gang aft agley', as they say.

This curriculum scenario has options; choices in other situations may be starker:

It was the start of the academic year. I had been put in charge of the site the year before, but it was quite run-down and depressing. Some of the staff felt I had sold them a dummy by agreeing to move there, but it gave them and me much more physical space and more autonomy. I had asked the chief executive for an upgrade to the buildings but been told there wasn't a snowball's chance. So I had timetabled the new year based on existing accommodation, which was fairly generous – at least I could avoid some of the more derelict spaces. Then, as I sat at my desk with ten minutes to start-time on the first day of the academic year, the phone rang. It was the local authority's Works Department manager. He had a fleet of painters available, and they would be arriving in an hour to plaster and re-paint half of my site.

My first reaction was: can you give me twenty-four hours? But the answer was negative: they started today or not all. No brainer. They had to come; and I had to find alternative accommodation for multiple groups instantly, and re-timetable the whole site within the day. Needless to say, it was done. Several weeks later, the building was transformed. Plans may have to be broken for the greater good.

Leaders cannot beat themselves up if things don't go 'according to plan'. They may have to invent new plans in the blink of an eye. This requires qualities such as flexibility, openness, the ability to see a bigger or longer-term picture (and sell it to hassled colleagues), and a malleability almost off the scale.

One boss for whom I worked said a wise thing: 'Maturity as a leader is measured by the degree of uncertainty you can live with'. Some days the uncertainty gets up and bites you: as a leader, are you ready?

★★★

This chapter has been about planning, and planning is usually for a change of practice. There is something you can rely on with respect to change: most people hate it, and many resist it either passively or actively (which, oddly, doesn't necessarily mean they will be discontent when the change becomes the new norm). Resistance, though, makes the role of the educational leader tricky at times.

Of course, a good leader will always try to take the team along, and will implement ideas that allow a careful transition from Point A to

Point B. But it would be fair to ask, what happens when someone will not play ball?

On one occasion as head of department, I wanted to encourage all my course leaders to produce an advertising and information brochure for their individual courses, in standard format for the institution, which would tell prospective students and those newly enrolled the key information about their chosen programme, for example:

- Course title
- Staff and their qualifications
- Validating body
- Rationale
- Outline syllabus
- Assessment procedures
- Important dates and deadlines
- Assessment criteria
- Potential job opportunities.

It wasn't exactly demanding stuff in today's world; and it was something which the course leader had to be fully aware of, and which they would implement constantly in their work. But one of my leaders refused point blank to undertake to provide parts of this information. They claimed that they did not believe that students should be party to things like detailed assessment criteria. For the leader, this knowledge was power, and revealing it would take away their 'expertise'.

Naturally, I had the obvious philosophical discussions with the leader, and I tried to explain the students' perspective on being in the dark about this kind of core information. But they were adamant. This presented a problem: I could lay down the law and insist, or I could act more subtly. Weighing the dangers in the former, I opted for the latter. But over the next few weeks I gradually set about requiring, piece by piece, the information that would make up this brochure. The course leader did not seem to realise what was happening and made no objection at all to letting me have the individual details I requested in random order. After a while I had a complete set of information and was able to explain to the leader that now all they needed to do was put it all into one document. No objection was raised, and all my course leaders now had parallel brochures. Maybe, too, there was a sudden realisation that not having a brochure disadvantaged the course when students were looking to make choices.

The motto of this story is: incrementalism can move mountains.

★★★

Some textbooks talk about planning as coming in three forms: operational, tactical, and strategic. This sounds a bit daunting, but it is really about timescales and the size of the stage on which the planning takes place.

- Strategic planning will mostly operate at the whole-institution level over a longer timespan.
- Tactical planning is about turning the strategic goals into intentions for a sub-unit such as a department, or a specialist subject area and may be medium-term planning.
- Operational planning relates to how those tactical intentions are, in turn, translated into what happens daily on the ground.

A common example might go something like this:

At the strategic level the head of a school wishes to improve the school's overall performance in public examinations at the end of next year. The head might put in place a student monitoring system so that every student's progress can be checked, perhaps by a deputy head, at regular intervals. This would act as an early warning of students who might be encouraged to perform better or who might not reach the levels required.

Departmental heads or year leaders, would operate at the tactical level, ensuring that they monitored at regular intervals, and acted on, the data collected to spot, and react to mitigate any deficiencies in the contribution of their area of work in the context of the overall performance of the institution. This might involve anything from interviewing students about under-performance to monitoring the competence of individual staff members.

But the people who delivered the result face-to-face with students, and who had to plan operationally to achieve this, would be the individual teachers.

★★★

Good planners need to be able to analyse problems in depth, focus attention on routes to solutions, and prioritise the order in which issues are tackled. Good leaders, having once planned, need effective communication skills to explain what is happening and why, and to encourage team ownership of the problem. Leaders need persistence to see things through, resilience when things go wrong, and the charisma to inspire others.

8

MARK TIME, SLOW TIME, QUICK TIME
Time as a leadership ally

**PERSONAL TIME   INSTITUTIONAL TIME
ORGANIZATIONAL TIME**

However we look at it, time is at the root of what we all do: in our professional lives, in our private lives, and in Life – it's the winged chariot aiming for one's back. We laugh at the figure of Onslow, sloth personified, in *Keeping Up Appearances* courtesy of Netflix, but there are two cautionary tales here. The first is that we are all guilty by reason of poor time management of wasting a lot of time. The second is that inefficiency in relation to time on the part of a leader is opportunity lost: ours as well as other people's.

There are just so many opportunities for time to leach away, like educational nutrients from the soil of learning under the torrent of busy-ness, that the leader must always be on his/her guard. Our staff may fail to plan learning and thus not deliver curriculum effectively. The discipline in the institution may become slack and open up lost moments of time in schools such as teachers dealing with behavioural issues rather than learning. Poor management may lead to the over-use of committees, or their deliberations may fail to result in, and act on, decisions. Leaders may be indecisive, staff may prevaricate about trivial issues, or students may be inadequately guided about how to study effectively.

As a footnote to indecision by educational leaders, how often have you heard the phrase 'we can't do anything until next term/next academic year'? What a travesty this is (especially when it's said on about 10 September!). Life, even educational life, is not bound by term dates, which are wholly artificial and serve only bureaucratic purposes. Thinking and learning operate independently of externally imposed schedules.

But how does one guard against this kind of problem? The answer is inevitably multilayered.

LAYER 1: START WITH YOURSELF

As a leader, you are the first link in the chain of command here. Begin by examining your own practice and the consequent example you set. How well do you make use of time?

Do you always arrive at work punctually? Early? When you arrive, are you fresh and ready to start the day with enthusiasm? Is your manner and body language alert and does it inspire confidence and eagerness in others? Are you available before formal sessions begin so that staff can bring you any queries or problems they may have about the day ahead? If they don't seek you out, do you seek some of them out each day to check on things you suspect might be issues for them, albeit very tactfully? Do you signal that you value these encounters as part of the life of the institution? If the people you manage are widely scattered, within a building or across campuses, do you make the effort to visit the far-flung individuals? Do you make it clear that each person's effort is also part of the team effort: we're all in it together?

Staff members in lowly positions in the overall hierarchy may feel marginalised unless the leader pays them some attention; and they, or others with lower self-esteem, may not understand the value of the work they do.

While I was quite new in one of my management roles I was supported by an office staff of four people: a senior administrator, a PA, a young man who kept an eye on financial transactions, and a newly appointed office junior (we'll call her Julie). One of the tasks I asked them to do was update me daily on any correspondence that went to them (rather than direct to me) which had implications I might need to know about for the day ahead. This task was delegated to Julie. The longer-serving staff knew I was always at my desk before them, so Julie was tasked with ringing me every morning with this information as early as was practical. Every day, my phone would ring and a voice would say: 'It's only me'. This grated on me because I wanted Julie to feel part of the team – my team. One morning when the phone went and the usual opening gambit was played, I said: 'No. It's not "ONLY you". It's YOU. You have a name. And for this moment of the day you are the most important person in my universe'. Later in the day, I passed through the admin office and there were a couple of funny looks. The senior officer said: 'Julie thought you were odd today; you said she was the most important person in the world'. I explained the daily ritual to colleagues and how I felt about the team of which we were all part. It was a moment of integration, after which hierarchies were largely forgotten and tasks became central and shared. We talked openly about everyone's individual and shared responsibilities; and the staff took the initiative to take up an offer of an independent review of practice within the team so we could work more effectively by playing to one another's strengths. This was a great time-saver because work became intuitive rather than compartmentalised. We trusted and appreciated each other more, too.

But, as a leader, you also need positive personal habits in relation to time. Keeping a diary (or some equivalent) is an obvious one. Habits are best kept simple. My preference is to use an A4 week-to-a-double-page diary, filled in manually (don't you just hate data-crashes and, even more, the people who mess up everyone else's lives because of them!). This kind of display has two strengths: you can view seven days' commitments at one glance (which may aid planning and scheduling), and the final space on the page is usually a blank for notes – I kept the diary as a constant companion whenever I was at my desk or in a meeting. Some may consider this approach very old-fashioned and not very 'modern' – that's fine. Though I am very computer-literate (I have taught higher degrees internationally using technology and am *au fait* with sophisticated photographic manipulation, for example), the fact remains – for ME – a manual system is more instantly accessible, quicker and more efficient: YOU are free to choose otherwise but make the choice based on usefulness not personal image.

The Notes section of my diary became my Bible for more effective use of time. As well as the teaching, meetings, and off-site tasks that governed my life, I could list in this 'eighth column' all those tasks which I wanted to shoe-horn into the week if time allowed (could have kept these data on my mobile or iPad). Two criteria conditioned which tasks got done: order of importance, and the time slot available – there's no point in starting a job, however important, that will take three hours if you only have 15 minutes: better to fit the task to the time and complete something properly. At the end of the week, anything outstanding got moved to the following double-page spread.

Everybody's life runs on slightly different clocks, but for me, throughout my working life, at least two hours a day were taken up with commuting. Wasted time? I would argue not. Here's why.

Work can be stressful, so we all need some down-time. Our best and most effective work comes after careful preparation and planning. For me commuting often gave me the opportunity to capitalise on both of these things. (It's worth interjecting here that driving always requires huge concentration and so I am not advocating driving in a reverie of work-related daydreams. Early in my life I became an advanced driver, and have sustained that skill throughout my life, teaching it to others too. Driving well and to the kind of systems advocated by the advanced motoring experts frees the mind to a degree from the tensions of driving.) After work, the drive home was a time when one could distance one's self from the pressures of the job and begin to move into a home-based mode. Before work, for some of the drive-time at least, one could mentally rehearse the key issues of the day so that one entered the workplace prepared for the first encounters. It worked for me – it may not work for you. You might prefer a run round the park, a session in the gym, a quiet beverage (not alcoholic if you're also driving), or a few minutes sitting on a bench in the park watching the world go by. But we all need to find our ploys for easing tension, quieting the spirit, and preserving our mental health.

On a slightly larger scale, beyond the day-to-day, it is important to take proper rests at weekends or during vacations. This doesn't mean you have to go to the Algarve and lie on a beach for six weeks with your eyes shut; it might be climbing a mountain, staying with your aunt for a few days, building a garden wall – whatever works for you. Choose your route – but the destination is down-time. This gets harder as the world becomes more e-conscious; but you can say 'No' at certain times and, if things get desperate, there is always the 'Off' switch.

To be a good leader requires personal time management of a high order. Only then can you turn your attention to time in other contexts.

LAYER 2: TAKE AN INSTITUTIONAL LOOK

A good leader will always be time-conscious, and that means being aware of where time is used efficiently and where it is lost. In whatever context the leader finds him/herself there is a need to be honest about time – within a department, across a team, within a whole institution, in the ways in which jobs are allocated and handled and carried through. Although an important caveat has to be: in educational contexts a good use of time does not always mean frenetic activity.

A nice, if fictitious, example of this is the recently remade French detective series *Maigret* with Rowan Atkinson, based on books by Georges Simenon. Maigret often appears detached, pipe-smoking and contemplative, but through reflection come inspiration, insight, revelation. So what follows does not undervalue reflection as a leadership process or as a means to improving learning.

In smaller schools, often primary schools, classes have a home-base room; and this is efficient in so far as time for getting out books, equipment, and so on is minimised. Large schools and colleges may have specific problems due to size and the need for specialised spaces; so students move from location to location several times a day. There are arguments for and against this practice, but it does need to be kept under control from a time-wasting perspective. Other movements in schools might include classes coming to and from a school assembly or meals, for example; and registration processes are often cumbersome. Some schools have abandoned 'playtimes' or 'breaks' because of their potential for time loss and also misbehaviour. Opinions are divided on these issues, with the decisions described as anything from 'a breath of fresh air' to 'inhuman', but as you move up the leadership ladder, you are going to have make an informed assessment of preferred practice and then implement it with the teaching team.

Some time-wasting is more subtle: pupils who are set tasks that are too easy for them may simply 'coast'; poorly differentiated work will exacerbate this issue; students might be given more opportunities to self-pace and make decisions about their own work. Examinations and assessments are seen by many as barriers to optimising learning time rather than (their intended purpose of) acting as useful boundary markers on the learning journey.

Perhaps the worst offender in the time-wasting category is poor student behaviour, which may be due to poor class management skills by (some) staff. One of the most extreme examples of this that I ever witnessed did not emanate from violent, rude, or aggressive behaviour by students, and seemed to me (as observer) to be happening in slow motion. I had been asked to deliver a day's in-service training at a large comprehensive school following an adverse Ofsted report, which I agreed to do on one condition: that I could spend a day in the school beforehand making my own assessment of what was going wrong. So I sat in on some lessons. The class of 25 Year 11 students was orderly enough when the lesson began, but the teaching was a bit pedestrian (though the science topic was potentially useful and interactive). Then a police helicopter began a sweep of the housing estate just across the school field. Gradually, every student, in ones and twos, left their seat and stood at the classroom windows watching the chopper. I waited to see what the teacher would do. The answer was nothing. Well, actually, she went on doing what she had been doing all along, except that now she was teaching the empty air: she was simply addressing the vacant seats without interrupting her flow. It was 15 minutes before the police abandoned the search and students wandered back to their benches. The teacher's lesson was a good one, but it delivered nothing to its intended audience.

Members of the teaching team can make their own lives easier by quite small adjustments of behaviour (though inexperienced members of staff might need some coaching in these ploys). For example, work for the week's classes can be planned in such a way that major outcomes which need to be marked are not set to every class taught within the same week, resulting in 500 projects to mark by next Friday. I always kept the student books that needed marking in piles on a table in order of urgency, so that spare moments could be taken up with keeping up with marking and I knew instantly where to begin.

Leaders need to be reviewing and sharing good practice within their departments or other areas of responsibilities. Part of the leader's job is to find and praise good practice, to support weaker individuals.

Middle managers are often better placed than senior leaders to identify and prompt colleagues about institutional problems of time wastage. But without doubt one role for leaders is to raise the awareness of the team regarding time-related issues.

LAYER 3: HOW TIME-SAVVY ARE YOUR STAFF?

When was the last time that you, as an education leader, organised training for staff on issues concerned with time management, or conducted an in-house audit (however informal) of how time was used across your area of responsibility or institution? Time is one of the most important factors in working successfully, and in maintaining a good mental approach to the job, yet it is one of the most neglected of all training needs. Poor time management is often a contributing factor in causing stress. Sartre commented wisely that the only one with time to rock the boat was the one who wasn't rowing; for leaders, under-occupied staff can be as much of an issue as the over-busy.

On taking up a new post, the first task I set myself was to procure some staff training about how to relieve stress: I judged that the teachers I had inherited were giving off negative vibes and needed to get a healthier perspective about their work. The trainer arrived and set about his task, but the more he identified strategies for less stressful working – including better use of time – the more uptight the audience became. His relaxed manner made them tense! So training may not be the way forward; if not, what is?

It's a longer-term goal, but establishing strategies that genuinely create time-gains, and give people more space for thinking, planning, activity, and recharging may be a better way.

There are a few things which, while fairly obvious, can help all educators. Before we start work on any task, it helps to have identified a clear purpose for the activity – what do other people (line manager, students) expect as a result of it, and what you yourself expect. One often hears people talking about 'fire-fighting', and that's the absolute opposite of what one hopes will be achieved. So thinking out the purpose and desired outcome for all aspects of our work will improve our mind-set. Planned action avoids being merely reactive. The acronym SMART was coined to aid this process. Our goals need to be:

- Specific
- Measurable
- Achievable
- Realistic
- Time-bound.

Working in this way presupposes a degree of planning and fore-thought, as identified earlier.

There are dangers, however. Some writers recommend tailoring one's lesson preparation time, for example, by using readily available online materials, That's fine provided they are of decent quality, and properly adapted to your purpose: too often they are not. I tried looking at some online materials about the Roman invasion of Britain for use with trainee teachers. They were very badly constructed, and often factually incorrect (did you know, for example, that the ancient Romans spoke Italian?), but they gave me a useful idea. I reproduced them. Then I asked the students to correct them by underlining in separate colours the things that were right, the things that were wrong, and the things that were half-truths. It proved a useful exercise. Similarly, be wary of using the same lesson with several parallel classes, or from year to year; the first person to be disillusioned by these tactics will be you!

Try to be creative. In preparing a tranche of material (never at the last minute, always thought about in advance), try to imagine several different in-roads into the material, so it is fresh for the students and fresh for you. The Government introduced PPA – time to be allocated to teachers within the working week specifically for preparing lessons and other non-contact tasks – but preparation goes beyond this allocated time; even on vacation one might find one's self taking some useful photographs of geological features in a landscape or of costume exhibits in a museum that might later inform one's classroom work.

When I first became a teacher-educator I used the mantra: teachers should be interesting and interested. If you are not interested in what you are doing then you are in the wrong job. If you don't demonstrate interest by your own knowledge, enthusiasm and energy, then you won't engage the students.

★★★

I see a lot of people at work in non-education roles. The thing that strikes me more and more is how much time they spend not actually working (i.e. doing something productive towards a planned objective). They chat, eat, and drink, and above all go online and either get involved in social media or games. They send countless e-mails about what I call 'Rosemary's baby' and are rarely on-task. Then they spend a lot of time telling anyone who will listen how busy they are, and how they don't have a slot in the diary big enough to do X – though they could have done X six times over in the time they have just wasted. Sorry, but we need a bit of honesty here.

One thing that will help staff use their time is to teach students how to use theirs more productively. If students can précis, take notes, use a variety of non-electronic media to gather information, measure out their own time on particular tasks in class and for home-work, self-check a portion of the work they have done, and become increasingly self-reliant then they are on the way to good learning habits and they will save staff time doing tasks that are unnecessary.

One other recurrent issue that militates against the effective use of time is untidiness. You have all seen those documentaries about army recruit training: how the newbies have to learn how to make beds, keep themselves clean, have everything folded in a regulation way, use their cupboard space tidily, polish their boots, and so on. You might think it is a waste of time. But it isn't. The discipline of doing these tasks well means that, when the chips are down, they know instantly where their kit is, it is ready for use, it is fit for pur-pose, and they can rely on its functioning correctly. This saves time and lives.

Now have a poke around some schools you know. The cleaners may be doing a good job, but the staffroom is full of used even mildewed cups, there are bits of PE kit on the floor as trip hazards, no one is quite sure who last used the laminator or where they stored the pouches, there's no paper in the duplicator and the secretary is off sick, and if you sit on a chair you might squash a student's GCSE project which is awaiting marking.

What did the Romans say: *Mens sana in corpore sano*? Which loosely translated means: if the place is a mess your professional life will be equally sloppy. It's down to the leader to see this isn't the case.

SOME BIGGER ISSUES OF TIME

As a school leader you will be involved not just in the in-house issues of educational thought and practice, but in debating and even implementing aspects of the bigger questions that affect the education system. The school calendar debate was an example of this.

Leaders quickly come to realise that people (even intelligent people in prominent positions) are often closed to any kind of change, even to thinking potential changes through without emotion. This happened a few years ago when I was working with Professor Brent Davies on an idea to abandon the rather dated three-term school system based on an agricultural economy and the Prayer Book calendar, and to replace it by five terms of equal length with two-week breaks except for a month's vacation in the summer. Though a tiny number of schools operated in this way, very successfully, there was massive resistance. One MP, seeing a main chance, did suggest to me that he might champion the cause provided it could be labelled as his idea, and twice I even had death threats! Vested interests prevailed. However, given the logic of the system, the local education authorities had to be seen to be doing something, so they invented the six-term year: you've guessed it — it was the old three-term year (which already had half-term breaks) relabelled. These debates are interesting, but leaders should never believe that they will win every battle, that good ideas will be warmed to, or that rivalries won't get in the way of educationally valuable change. Realism is one of the most important aspects of leadership.

Brent and I also worked with schools in the UK and overseas which were experimenting with different kinds of school day. Imagine you have a school which is too small to cope with the number of students in the area who wish to attend it. One solution might be to do what a Portuguese comprehensive did: invent a three-session day. The school operated morning, afternoon, and evening sessions. Staff and students were allocated to ten sessions in total (i.e., the same workload as before), but over the course of a week might work three mornings, five afternoons, and two evenings. This meant that the operating costs of the school were reduced for the local authority, all those who wanted them got places, and some staff, at least, enjoyed this more flexible approach to employment. Though such systems are not widely adopted in the UK, their influence appears in things like breakfast and homework clubs, and extended school days that allow students to use the facilities outside conventional operating hours, which may have social benefits.

Using school time in more flexible ways makes sense when provision is so costly. Leaders need to develop the kinds of malleable and imaginative thinking that can cope with changing circumstances in an uncertain world.

★★★

Time is an important phenomenon in life and school life; educational leaders need to keep it constantly under scrutiny and master it rather than be mastered or worn down by it. This chapter has not exhausted the possibilities of the subject, nor trawled all the debates, but it has thrown up some pointers for leaders about the range of issues that use of time affects. I spend some of my leisure time teaching people the skills of advanced driving. One of these is to produce a drive which, in my words, contains light and shade. I encourage the candidate to think about the pattern of the drive: moments when we are at rest; the movement up through the gear-box to drive through the town within the 30mph speed limit; the increase in acceleration as appropriate when we leave the built-up area and head into National Speed Limits of the country lanes; the smooth loss of speed suitable for corners or bends on the route; and maybe the full-stop of a traffic light on red. This light and shade, carefully handled, is a mark of skill; and it is no different in the life of a leader.

There are moments when it is entirely appropriate to mark time – in other words to let the status quo prevail – usually because things are going quite well and other, more important, issues need to be given priority. That's fine; the team needs stability and the leader is freed to concentrate on other things.

There are moments when a slow march is the right pace for the changes we need to make in order to improve practice on matters such as time management. Rushing into making changes when they are not thought-through, or when the team is not psychologically or logistically prepared to do a proper job, is unwise; maybe a few incremental steps are enough as a first shot.

But there are moments when the leader needs to take control and prompt a rethink of practice and the improvement of practice: to encourage the quick march of progress. This is the time for providing the vision, the support, the commands, the inspiration, the heightened morale that the team will need to cross the next hurdle and achieve the objective.

9

BECOMING ÉLITE: DEVELOPING AND FURTHERING YOUR SKILLS

Stand still to drop dead: The need to advance your leadership skills and career

PROFESSIONAL DEVELOPMENT LEARNING FROM RESEARCH

I am going to start this chapter by getting on my high horse. This is a chapter about *you* but… I hope by now you have realised that everything that has been said in this book is really about *students* – about doing the best for *them*, making *their* work interesting, improving *their* life chances, setting *them* on the path to future well-being. This came home forcibly to me when I was on a study and research visit in Portugal. We were taken into the atrium of a large secondary school. The Portuguese are famed for their ceramics, and the students had decorated the atrium walls with a huge tiled picture of a teacher; a bespectacled Mr Chips caricature. But it wasn't the picture that was striking, it was the legend underneath it: '*Ser professor e dar se*', it read – To be a teacher is to give *yourself*.

So, although this chapter is about *your* professional development, it is also about the real beneficiaries: your students, your colleagues, and your institution. To pick up on the military metaphors, this chapter is about you becoming an élite performer; and we think instantly about the SAS, the Paras, the Commandos; but also about specialist units like Engineers. And we think, too, about special individuals who distinguish themselves in the cause of others, like Private (now

Sergeant) Johnson Beharry VC COG. His self-sacrifice is captured in accounts of his action on 1 May 2004. Beharry was driving a Warrior armoured vehicle, called to assist an ambushed foot patrol. The vehicle was hit by multiple rocket propelled grenades, sustaining damage. Radio communications were lost. The platoon commander, the vehicle's gunner, and a number of other soldiers in the vehicle were injured. The periscope optics were damaged and Private (as he then was) Beharry was forced to open his hatch to steer his vehicle, exposing his face and head to a torrent of small arms fire. Beharry drove through the ambush, leading five other Warriors to safety. He extracted his wounded comrades from the vehicle, all the time exposed to enemy fire and wounded. He was awarded a Victoria Cross for valour of the highest order.

★★★

An *Independent* article claimed that élite forces are some of the best-trained and most formidable… they go where others fear to tread. Calling the best school leaders élite makes me smile because it reminds me of my first promoted post (i.e. one that came with extra money!), which required me to work with two other staff to educate a group of 75 disaffected school-leavers in a London secondary modern. We split them into three classes sometimes, but often one of us would teach the whole group while the others prepared new curriculum or arranged visits to places of interest (an effective use of time). These kids had a reputation, but it wasn't a good one. Advisory staff and school inspectors from miles around used to come to see how one teacher could teach 75 of them, alone, for a whole afternoon. One visitor actually said to me: 'How the hell do you do that?' I didn't tell him: he didn't need to know, as they say in élite circles (but you may have worked it out as you have read this book).

★★★

How can leaders improve the effectiveness of their leadership, become the élite among leaders, even train other leaders? At some stage in your leadership career you will almost certainly want, and/or be encouraged, to pursue a higher degree (Master's) in some aspect of leadership. That's fantastic, but let's clear some other ground first.

I always want to go back to a fundamental principle when I talk about higher education (HE), and the principle is: this is an arena where intelligent people come with open minds to explore the best solutions to (shared) problems with every idea up for debate.

But before you get as far as HE, you may be tempted by courses and conferences widely offered in the profession and on the internet, so, a few words of caution. 'Official' qualifications that come with a kind of seal of government approval may be good as far as they go, and they may even be a required stepping-stone. But be a bit wary. They often require their graduates to speak in officialese and hold accepted opinions. If you must, progress through the hurdle, but keep your thinking your own and be true to yourself. (At this point, I can hear the political artillery moving forward and ranging their guns to shoot me down – but that is an honest opinion based on evidence. As someone who trained via a perfectly competent course to be an Ofsted inspector, I can say from experience that freedom of thought didn't top the agenda. Participation in inspection confirmed my misgivings.)

Conferences are a bit of a mixed bag. Covid-19 has perhaps done the profession a favour by helping to raise awareness of other ways of doing things than simply packing people into a lecture hall and running through a succession of speakers. There IS a place for this, but there are key questions you should ask yourself before getting involved in this kind of training, such as:

- Is the theme right for me in my situation?
- Will the outcomes improve my professional thinking and analysis?
- Will they improve my classroom skills?
- Will I increase my knowledge as a result?
- How and to what extent will this benefit my students?
- How effective is the speaker (use reputation, research on the internet)?
- How/to what extent will this benefit my school?
- Is there a more (time/money) economic way of getting the same experience?

It is probably as important to read as to undertake the traditional once-a-year conference experience. Your subject organisation will produce a journal: the Historical Association is a good example in humanities, with its journal *Teaching History*, and the *School Science Review* serves a similar purpose in science. You could also become actively involved in the organisation, which is a good way to broaden horizons and make contacts. There are also on-line opportunities for training using sites such as *Teachmeet* and *researchEd* – though the same caveats apply as to conferences, and they come down to this: target your time for maximum benefit. Remember: there is more than a single strand to your professionalism: teaching skills, of course; subject knowledge and update; and professional skills such as leadership, time-management, curriculum analysis, and so on. All of these strands need to be on your training agenda. Open University (OU) courses have always been a good investment, and the OU offers a versatile selection of free-standing modules. Many of these options have the opportunity for colleagues to get together and form their study groups within their own schools or clusters (we return to in-house research a bit later). This kind of experience may whet your appetite for more sustained study at Master's level.

★★★

A Master's degree in leadership is a *sine qua non* for top leaders so in what follows I am going to talk you through three things: how to go about selecting a course; what some good courses look like; and why some training may not be effective on the ground. After you have been a middle leader for a while, this is the logical next step towards senior leadership.

SELECTING A MASTER'S DEGREE IN LEADERSHIP

Selecting a Master's in education leadership can be quite bewildering, and since either you or your employer is going to spend a lot of money on it, and you are going to invest your time, a right choice becomes important. There are some very basic things you can clear out of your thinking quite early on.

These qualifications come with a variety of outcomes: commonly, MA, MA(Ed), MSc, MBA, MPhil. There are differences between these, but HE institutions don't standardise their practice, so they are pointers rather than rules. MPhil is usually regarded as the top end of the Master's continuum because it is research-based rather than 'taught' – i.e. about learned content – but one or two universities buck the trend, so be wary. MBAs are again at the top end of the spectrum, but may have a content which is skewed towards those with business concerns – finance, particularly; they are good for school administrators but not universally useful for teacher-leaders. Some universities use the MSc designation to try to make the award a bit more up-market than an arts degree, but it doesn't mean that the degree has any real scientific content; though there are exceptions in the sense that some MSc degrees do have a high research content even though they are not exclusively research-based degrees. The most common Master's appellations are MA and MA(Ed), the latter, one assumes, to avoid the dreaded 'bought MA' tag associated with Oxbridge; these are usually, but not always, taught rather than strong on research.

Let's begin by looking at the MA, MA(Ed), MSc cluster of qualifications and deal with the MPhil later (MBAs probably won't concern you). More important than the actual 'letters' is the content of the degree, so the advice is: collect as many prospectuses as you can and then read them very carefully – they are widely available on the internet. If you are going for a taught option (as opposed to research only) match your choice with a content that meets your needs and an organisation that fits your availability and lifestyle. (Remember, online prospectuses are adverts: treat them all with appropriate scepticism.)

Once you have narrowed the field on these bases, look at the staff list. Try to assess whether the calibre, experience, and interests of the staff members match what you would want in your tutors. Simplistically, if you work in a primary school and the staff all have secondary or HE backgrounds, then the chances of your feeling empathy with the taught elements may be limited. If you want to study leadership, don't choose a department which is predicated on management.

WHAT A LEADERSHIP MASTER'S DEGREE MIGHT LOOK LIKE

The likely composition of the degree will be a number of 'taught' modules. These will probably be assessed by a series of research-based assignments embedded in your own work in your own institution; and then you will be required to write an extended piece of work (20,000-word dissertation) which is also research-based on a topic of your own choosing about leadership in your context. If the degree does not follow this kind of pattern, be wary. You can read content out of a book at any time cheaply without following a degree course; engagement with the material in a practical way through the research elements is critical to improving your skill and understanding (insight) as opposed to your knowledge. *A propos* of nothing much, the other day a young acquaintance of mine who is preparing for university next year said: 'My teachers are quite nice people, and some of them obviously love their subjects; but they are all boring – they have no idea how to share their enthusiasm'. They would probably blame the imposed curriculum, but they'd be wrong. If they went on an MA in teaching skills, you'd expect them to teach better; if you choose an MA in leadership, people will expect you to lead better.

One further criterion by which to assess a potential course is the degree to which it allows you to make choices. Adult education – and supremely, education for highly qualified and talented individuals – needs to allow them to be in the driving seat. A heutagogical approach – beginning from where the adult learner is and following a track that meets their immediate needs – has to have learning advantages[1]. If you can, find people who have followed your potential route, talk to them in depth. Ask especially about the quality and availability of supervision. Your investment in a couple of cappuccinos will be worthwhile!

An MPhil degree dispenses with the shorter assignments (in most instances) and demands a research dissertation of about 40,000 words on a topic selected by the candidate and approved by the university. For anyone with some research background and knowledge, say in a related field, this can be a genuinely interesting option, but it is not where most leaders start. If you contemplate this option, seek advice from the potential tutors: it might be a lonely road for the unsuspecting. Nonetheless, the inevitable connection between leadership and continued learning was recognised by the late John F. Kennedy himself: 'Leadership and learning are indispensable to each other'.

WHY A LEADERSHIP MASTER'S DEGREE MAY NOT CHANGE ANYTHING IN YOUR SCHOOL

A recent *Harvard Business Review* article explored the uncomfortable fact that training often fails to deliver its intended results, however. Too often training is carried out in isolation, and the newly trained person has no one to relate to and no agenda to follow when the training is over. Training an individual doesn't alter an organisation. Organisations are organic; picking out an isolated individual or unit does not impact on the wider institution. Training for a leader is likely to work best when the senior management team (SMT) knows what it wants from that process, and can contextualise the outcome to its clearly stated mission and values for the organisation: if the mission and values are not clear, then the training will fail. Fractured SMTs will not improve an organisation by training, and an organisation where senior managers don't share trust with their middle leaders will never persuade the leaders to confide in them about where the blockages in the organisation are. Many organisations have no system for rewarding leadership talent when it happens, and they thus lower motivation.

Despite the problems, many leaders do use the HE system to further their expertise, and they do increase their own confidence and bring a wider palette of skills to the organisation. You can, and will, benefit yourself and others by joining this élite.

★★★

There are related activities which can expand your training horizons in leadership. None of them come without a penalty of time and commitment, but they are all potentially valuable and interesting.

DOCTORAL WORK

If you get bitten by the academic bug you might want to take your studies on to doctoral level. There are two kinds of doctoral work, both very demanding: the professional doctorate (often called EdD) and the fully research-based degree (PhD). It is not the place here to discuss their merits but much of what has already been said applies.

IN-HOUSE RESEARCH

Some schools encourage in-house research. Groups of interested staff get together to solve a problem using the tools of research. An example might be:

As subject leader you discover that many students do not enjoy the current curriculum in Aramaic (I chose a dead language simply so as to make the example generic): the work is difficult, their enthusiasm is low, and results in examinations are poor. Yet both students and parents expect this subject to be successful as they see it as an important career option.

You and your colleagues agree that the situation needs to change; and that it might be worthwhile to probe it as deeply as possible – it is the ideal piece of small-scale research. The research questions include:

- What precisely do students see as the problems with the subject as it is currently taught?
- What do students feel could be improved in the delivery of the teaching?
- What curriculum changes might ease the difficulties students have?
- Do any changes to teaching and curriculum improve student results?
- Do improved delivery of the subject and better results make students' attitudes more positive?

The staff agree on a set of interview questions to begin to answer the first two research questions, and delegate a member of staff to interview a representative sample of the Aramaic group.

The results from this survey are used to remodel the curriculum, and all the teaching staff work on this, and agree how to present it with new teaching techniques.

The new curriculum and teaching approaches are trialled over the next few weeks. Assessment test results are scrutinised for improvements.

At the end of term, the staff hold a round-table or focus group discussion with the students to assess their reactions to the new teaching methods and the curriculum.

This low-key, small-scale research has many advantages: staff and students both feel listened to and involved; things change, hopefully for the better; parents see their views are important; results improve; teachers have more job satisfaction.

If you get the chance to participate in this kind of work or lead an investigation it can be a great collaborative learning experience. Table 9.1 shows some kinds of research that teachers and leaders can involve themselves in.

Table 9.1 Types of research carried out by teachers

Type of research	Example	Value
Case study	Most teachers carry out a case study at some time – they may look at a job role (such as pastoral care) or the use of a new teaching space.	Of immediate value in the workplace, with potential for sharing professional knowledge with colleagues as well as for influencing one's own performance.
Statistical studies	An analysis of SATs or GCSE/A level scores over time.	Can provide hard evidence of trends and alert the school to potential problems and remedial action.
Curriculum research	Usually the devising and trialling of a new piece of subject curriculum.	Has potential value for self, colleagues, and pupils.
Evaluation studies	A form of case study designed to take an innovation and subject it to scrutiny, e.g. the effectiveness of a new merit system.	May help to throw up issues, e.g. the bias towards girls of merits awarded, or the uneven effect on pupils where some teachers operate the system and some don't.
Child development studies	Need stringent confidentiality, but the study of individual children over time – e.g. those with special needs – may help to identify improved remediation.	Practical value for pupils, and for feedback to parents; but must be handled ethically.
Linguistic analysis	A study of children's writing to discover their access to a range of forms.	Designed to improve teaching and learning through the teacher's greater insight.

WRITING

Eventually you will want to communicate your research findings to others. Start modestly by producing a short paper for a staff meeting or the department staff. You might then want to branch out into writing for a magazine or journal that produces what are, in effect, summaries of research activity: a good example would be the journal *Impact* from the Chartered College of Teaching[2]. Later, you may consider contributing a full-blown research item for a refereed journal in your field. The journals themselves are very good at informing authors about the journal's requirements on content and format and, of course, you will have trawled through the back issues online, but in the early days you might find it useful to get help from a colleague who has been through the process and can act as a critical reader.

CONSULTANCY

If you become sufficiently expert in a leadership field, it is not impossible that you may be in demand to train colleagues in other schools on a consultancy basis. This is also a great learning opportunity; you can never see too much of other people's practice.

★★★

I believe in evolution and the implication for all of us is that, if we fail to evolve and progress we will simply fail and become extinct. Growing in our role, growing into a new role, continuing growth is what makes you as a leader part of an élite. The prerequisite of that growth is to know what you are growing towards: the vision, the mission. On that, every leadership guru in the world agrees. For education leaders, the path towards the mission is diverse and needs many skills. One of those skills is constant updating, training, observing, and drawing out of resultant lessons. Research is one of the tools through which this can happen, through which your leadership can grow.

As you grow, you will grow your confidence and your integrity. Your staff, your students will know that what they see in you is what they get, and what they get they can rely on. An account in Nanson's book holds the mood: after a day's engagement, the officer in charge addressed the men. He accepted they were in a difficult position. Without Churchillian heroics he was able to convey calm and a spirit of togetherness. This approach raised morale. The tone of the operation changed.

10

LEADERS IN CONTEXT
Leadership across institutional styles

CHARISMATIC BUREAUCRATIC LAISSEZ-FAIRE TRANSACTIONAL TRANSFORMATIONAL

For decades the image of outstanding leadership in schools, and more generally, accorded instantly with the Great Person theory – and what these individuals had, it was believed, was charisma. So, in preparation for writing this chapter on leadership style I thought I ought to begin from this classic position.

How can one sum up the Great Person theory? Because it is featured repeatedly on television, especially in the Christmas period, most of the country's population has, I guess, seen the film *Zulu*, set in the days of Empire in Africa. Lieutenant Chard took charge of the impossible and succeeded against the odds. The action saw the award of the largest number of VCs ever (before or since) for one engagement; each side saluted the bravery of the other. Chard is the epitome of charisma. Charismatics achieve great, sometimes seemingly impossible things. In popular opinion, positive charismatics include, for example, Mother Theresa, Martin Luther King, Archbishop Tutu and Michelle Obama. Jesus, of course, whether he was or was not divine, kick-started a world movement that has survived for 2,000 years so, clearly, he had some rare quality: similar claims could be made for other religious leaders. But charisma fell out of favour. In schools, anyway, no one wanted (often rightly) to accord a head teacher heroic status or the sole credit for successes.

But there is another side to the debate. As a result, I was prompted to write a short article in defence of charisma. Basically, my argument whittled down to this: the charismatic leader comes into his/her own in a crisis. When a school or other organisation is hit by a wall of trouble, often it takes one person with clear insight, physical endurance, massive courage, and total determination to rescue it – back to a metaphorical Rorke's Drift. However, once the situation has been rescued, the charismatic leader needs to reframe his/her thinking and relinquish that total control at all costs (lest they burn out), to find a way of reassigning aspects of leadership by means of delegation. One doctoral thesis which I examined explained how the four head teachers studied had sacrificed their health, their marriages, their leisure time, and their whole way of life to the cause of running their respective schools. The charismatic leader role may be too uncomfortable as a long-term proposition but, in some circumstances, these charismatics need to be valued and their achievement recognised. If your back is to the wall you might need a charismatic or to find your own charisma. In the real world, this is the realm of leadership in failing schools or failing departments. The charismatic resonates with all those virtues like courage, determination, resilience, which we discussed earlier.

★★★

If the charismatic model of school leadership has romantic undertones, the bureaucratic model generally raises a yawn. Based on the work of the sociologist Max Weber, bureaucracies are associated with formal rules and procedures; long and rigid personal and institutional hierarchies; slowness to change; division of labour; a philosophy of 'one size fits all'. Allegedly espousing meritocracy and the promotion of the talented they may, in reality, safeguard structural privileges. Bureaucracies thrive on notions like hierarchy, specialisation, and standardisation. For example, one of the crimes I hold bureaucracy accountable for in my lifetime has been the move to separate the learning function of teachers from the counselling one as part of the notion of specialisation. Teaching is about the whole person, not about selected bits of them.

You may well be thinking at this point: none of that reflects my approaches to life and work. But be wary of smugness here. Bureaucracy is insidious. For example, the English (I'm not so sure about the Celts) have an in-built tendency to accept hierarchy and order: 'I was first in this queue, she was second, he was third, they were fourth…' On the other hand, if someone does queue-jump, most people are too polite to yell 'Oi mate, I was first'. It would disturb our social niceties, you see.

Given our temperament, it is not hard to see how bureaucracy can creep into and overwhelm school life. You think that the school needs a policy about (let's choose something neutral) Velcro-fastening footwear. The head isn't enthralled by this disturbance, which smacks too much of thinking in the ranks, and maybe has hints of future subversion and power-grab. But as a self-styled democrat he is required to be seen to act. So he asks the policy committee to set up a policy sub-committee to discuss the merits or otherwise of Velcro-fastening footwear. He puts his loyal deputy in the chair of that committee. It meets endlessly, but never actually reaches a resolution. At an Ofsted inspection a year down the line, part of the school's paperwork reads: 'We set up appropriate committees to explore controversial issues like Velcro-fastening footwear, and these are currently active in investigating the issues'. After the inspection, the Velcro sub-committee continues to meet for another six months at the end of which it has produced a resolution to make a resolution within the next 12 months and you have a new job in another school. Bit of a caricature? Only just!

But that example is the micro-level of bureaucracy (and remember, I said earlier in this text that administration is not the same as bureaucracy – all organisations need a base-line level of administration). At the macro-level, bureaucracy has more to answer for. For the past two decades, governments have assumed that measurements and scores are the way to assess how well a school is doing. This view is so entrenched that (with complete illogicality) almost every measure of social difference in the intake make-up of pupils is ignored in order to serve the simple rule of testing, i.e. that one size can be applied as a measure of intellectual performance for all. The bureaucratic approach to schools resonates with the view of society that treats individuals like automata: people have their place in a hierarchy that is effectively fixed, that hierarchy extends out of school into society; people can do only the things prescribed as appropriate to them and their place in the world, which is preordained. As an aside here, I was once introduced to a self-styled education expert; she said: 'Oh someone with that name writes books'. 'That's me', I said. 'Really!' She said, 'You don't look like someone who writes books'.

In the future it may be that an electronic/information world will make some aspects of bureaucracy redundant (e.g. people will have more and varied access to knowledge as and when they want it) or it may enslave more completely (by removing some of their social interaction and replacing it with 'acceptable' information delivered without the immediate intervention of sentient beings). If you think this last is far-fetched, look at our shopping habits: fewer and fewer of us make a journey to the high street shops, have conversations with real operatives, pick and choose goods by touch and sight and so on; instead we look on a machine, order with electronic clicks, receive goods by a courier who is detached from the supplier, and tick a box relating to satisfaction levels. If bureaucracy is about the dehumanisation process, most of us are well down the road. And if you thought that an organisation run by a charismatic might be unhealthy, how about one run by a bureaucrat? Or a robot?

★★★

But in response to those last questions, maybe I have the perfect answer for your incipient fears: the laissez-faire (LF) leader. I worked for one – not in a school but in a teacher education environment – and I decided to research the effects of the LF model in some depth.

The LF leader is a 'hands-off' practitioner operating in a notionally collegiate style. Like other leadership styles, the delegative approach has both a number of benefits and shortcomings. Sometimes this style can be effective, particularly if it is used appropriately in the right settings and with groups that respond well, and on a short-term basis. LF leadership of an institution or organisation can be deemed appropriate when the section leaders are themselves more expert than their boss. In theory, then, the section leaders can just get on with the job with minimum supervision; the resulting independence is felt by section leaders to be liberating and they can indulge their passion for the joint venture in their own contexts. This approach to leadership requires a great deal of mutual trust.

But nothing is ever that simple. Missions, visions, or projects are best served when the journey towards them is co-ordinated, albeit with a light touch. Hands-off approaches fail in most cases to set the deadlines, manage the feedback, and create the group cohesion that a shared project requires to succeed. The boss is often seen as lacking competence, short on confidence, or even a proper interest in, or commitment to, his/her own project. He/she may be perceived as failing to be personally accountable and merely using the section leaders as scapegoats. One, more extreme, view holds that LF leaders 'represent passivity or even an outright avoidance of true leadership. In such cases, these leaders do nothing to try to motivate followers, do not recognize the efforts of team members, and make no attempts at involvement with the group'[1].

Other, more detailed, research concluded: 'laissez-faire leadership may be more of a counterproductive leadership style than a zero type of leadership style'[2].

In my own research for a Master's degree in leadership, I discovered that my fellow section leaders claimed that what was alleged to be a collegiate style of leadership was often 'authoritarian, non-consultative, and lacking in a willingness to hear advice'. They said that their reservations about quality in the project were not taken seriously, and the stress resulting from this was ignored. The boss would not face resource issues. In carrying out this research, I collected all the e-mailed directives I had received from the boss over a significant period (more than 100 items); some of my colleagues sent me items about the same issues. Two documents that particularly struck a note of dissonance were directives on exactly the same subject, written on the same day, to me and to another section leader by our boss. One said diametrically the opposite of the other. In the real world of leadership action, these two documents could have put the two section leaders in aggressive opposition to one another. This intended conflict can be a feature of LF management. In this case, the boss was not aware of the extent to which the section leaders literally compared notes.

★★★

Two other leadership styles commonly discussed with respect to schools are the transactional and the transformative. Before we look at these, though, a caveat. You will find, among the theorists, a plethora of labels for leadership styles. Which are in vogue tends to have more to do with fashion than anything more tangible. However, do not assume that each model stands as a discrete and separate entity; they merge, blend, get used together in different circumstances or towards different groups of people. All these labels do is to act as convenient clothes-pegs with which to shorthand a dominant approach within a given organisation.

Transactional leadership is often associated with qualities such as supervision, organisation, and performance. Transactional leaders may show symptoms of the charismatic and the bureaucratic in their behaviour. I suspect that, in the early days of Academies, most Academy principals fell into this category. The first Academies were marked out as schools where performance was exemplary; this level of performance was typically achieved on the back of a huge drive by every subject area to excel, with students scoring up to 20 GCSE passes with many of the grades at A or A⋆, and a similar outstanding standard maintained into GCE examinations. Heads of department and subject leaders were certainly under pressure to achieve these results. Just as principals put pressure on leaders, so leaders put pressure on staff to sustain these levels. Every student's performance was monitored, at least half-termly. Remedial action was taken for students who were under-performing against these criteria. The same kinds of standards were often applied to non-examination work. Student shortcomings were often used as evidence of staff inadequacies, so a deputy head might be appointed to oversee under-performing staff members. These academies had top-down models of management and were hierarchical in organisation.

In the scenario described you can see how performance, organisation and supervision worked together to produce an ethos. The news was not all bad, and the results were often exceptional. The organisation and supervision often meant these academies were places where there was little time lost to poor student behaviour, and issues like poor attendance were minimised. There were, however, examples where even the buildings felt slightly oppressive. I remember visiting one such institution which had evolved out of a troubled comprehensive where the rooms for senior staff were so planned into the new building that they gave views over all corridors and stairwells so as to give early alert of any misbehaviour.

By contrast, if the transactional approach includes both positive and negative reinforcement, transformational leadership emphasises positives such as motivation and inspiration. Transformational leadership still sets clear goals, but it is unlikely these goals will be solely determined by outside agencies such as levels of examination success. On the route to those goals, the leader will provide positive qualities such as support, encouragement, and recognition to both staff and students. High expectations feature in schools run by transformational leaders and they are achieved through encouragement and the leader's ability to inspire. Transformational organisations may attract strong emotional support from their personnel. Leaders will tend more towards adopting teamwork, collegiality, and the selection of common goals as opposed to individual success. There is less of the Great Man/Woman about this kind of leadership. A good leader is someone who, when the job is done, makes their followers aware that *they* have done it.

★★★

In this chapter I have only scratched the surface of a few of the theoretical approaches to leadership often referred to in the academic literature. The discussion has been raised here with the major intention of alerting you not just to your own leadership style, but to encourage you to understand the context within which you yourself are led.

Having given you the flavour of the debates and put them in settings which I hope are practical, my intention is to continue the discussion only by referring you to some of the vast literature in this field[3]; if you decide to take up the idea of a Master's degree in leadership you will spend time on these models as part of your reading and understanding.

While working in a university Leadership Department, I had a discussion with a colleague who was talking about supervising school leaders on the doctoral route. He asked me whether I felt that, to be a trainer in this field one ought to have been a leader in a school. My response was that I didn't think it could, or should, be otherwise. It transpired that he had no such experience and thought all that mattered was the generation of sound theory. My former colleague would see this book as the antithesis of that. The stance of this text has been that theory is fine as a way of refining thinking about leadership, but leadership becomes a reality only when it is lived – i.e. based in what is practical and doable. Theories of leadership are good and useful if all you do is write books about them, but leadership itself is something that has to be lived 'on the ground' among real people in real situations. Now, the judgement about that debate is yours.

You are reaching the end of this book, but maybe only a waypoint on your leadership journey: once a leader, always a leader. You now must decide how to take things forward. What do you want out of it for the rest of your career?

11

SWIFT AND BOLD
Completing your leadership journey

AMBIGUITY   THE FUTURE   TIMING

Earlier in the book I told you that I was an Army cadet in my youth, badged to the King's Royal Rifles. The regiment itself had almost ceased to exist because, like so many other historical regiments, it was amalgamated at that time (into the Royal Green Jackets); its more recent incarnation is The Rifles. The Regiment was raised in 1756 in America, and the soldiers were fast-moving skirmishers whose purpose was to move in ahead of the heavier infantry to harass the enemy. The regiment was distinctive: the cap badge was black (rather than shiny brass, which may have glinted in the sun and given the soldier's position away); it was prophetically (since I have had so much to do with training education leaders on the Island) in the shape of a Maltese Cross. Its motto ran: *Celer et audax = Swift and bold*. The riflemen march faster than other infantry regiments: 140 paces to the minute instead of 120. I always felt the motto was a good one: it had something to say more widely about an approach to life.

★★★

You are approaching the end of this book. It has been a book about leadership in which I have used some of my own experiences and those of my colleagues, and examples from my own employment, to focus your attention on the leader's roles. But it is, nevertheless, a book about your leadership: how you can review your skills, improve your performance, and expand your future in the endlessly fascinating context of education. It is your journey, and I just want to remind you of some of the waypoints on it.

In Chapter 1 you saw how education leaders emerge from the wider professional body, you considered the roles of both followers and leaders, and how emergent leaders are noticed because of their ability to inspire. In the second chapter you noted the differences between the organisational and procedural focus of managing, and the intention of leaders to change people and practices; you began to understand that self-discipline is another hallmark of leadership. Though it is difficult to acknowledge, you saw in Chapter 3 how all leaders fail sometimes; you noted that this can result in stress, and that to counteract stress you have to develop resilience, which in turn results in increased confidence.

Having resolved to push onwards on the leadership journey, in Chapter 4 you used your confidence to adopt positive characteristics: an approach through quality, how to inspire others towards a vision and mission, and self-belief. Team working was the theme of Chapter 5, acknowledging that where possible you, as the leader, do not have to be a lone or lonely figure, but can find a view of inclusiveness in your teams even through the notion of allowable weakness. But as leader, you can never abdicate your responsibilities and, as Chapter 6 indicates, one of those is leading from the front when necessary; for which purpose you need to develop independence and courage. At the heart of the leadership journey is planning, and in Chapter 7 you were introduced to the SMEALCS planning system, and through it revisited in more detail the vision and mission concepts of earlier chapters.

By Chapter 8 you were beginning to realise that keeping the concept of time onside as an ally would help your leadership; and you looked at personal time management, institutional time management, and some of the bigger questions of time usage that beset the education system. You moved on in Chapter 9 to consider the ways in which you might polish your leadership skills: to become an élite leader. Finally, in Chapter 10 you reviewed some more theoretical models of how institutions are led, and at the pros and cons of these systems.

★★★

This brief volume has tried to be inspirational and yet immediate. Before signing off, however, one ought to spend a few moments speculating about future change. Clearly leaders, teachers, and students are having their world of school altered by access to information technology; elsewhere I have discussed some of the issues that relate to the ethical usage of e-learning. But these same, or related, technologies are changing the world from which our students come: they have the potential to spread false information, to drive the less robust into fantasy worlds, they are already lowering human capacity to make face-to-face relationships. Technology provides the option of globalisation, but, despite the latter's strengths, there are already serious doubts about the loss of distinctiveness which is the outcome. Education is concerned with the growth of the whole person, and this cannot fully flourish in the face of learning which is heavily reliant on computer technology. The same issues burrow, perhaps even further, into our non-educational lives: think how Alexa has transformed simple daily tasks and consider the implications of this for transforming human behaviour. The IT world is, of itself, neutral, but the uses to which it is put may not be. We are already under involuntary scrutiny by the state, by big business, and even in trivial things like shopping for everyday goods. At some point the machine will control the person. What are education leaders doing to protect future generations in a world which is instant, exciting, and yet subject to serious, potentially malign, persuasion?

★★★

This has been your journey, and my hope is that you consider it to have been worthwhile, provocative, and, at times, even fun. Of course, you don't have to agree with every opinion expressed in the book: the opinions are mine, the journey is yours. Nor do you have to model your journey on mine, or your leadership style on the approach which you have deduced from this text might be mine: leadership should evolve constantly as the world changes, and no two days are the same. But we do well to remember that every journey leads somewhere; Weidenhall described journeys of birds on migration as weaving an 'incredible tapestry'; and our leadership can weave a tapestry in the lives we touch: students' or staff. Take from this text whatever you have found positive. Certainly, you will have seen that many aspects of leadership are shared, they are not yours or mine exclusively; and handling that ambiguity is part of the journey too.

But I think the rifleman's motto has much to commend it to education leaders on a day-to-day basis: *Celer et audax*. In Chapter 8 we discussed the use of time; but in decision-making TIMING is just as important and more immediate. Delay, and the opportunity dies; act too soon and the impact is lost and you give yourself away. *Celer et audax*: when you have made up your mind *to act*, do it quickly and cleanly without indecision. When you take your decision about *how to act*, do it boldly.

> May Zeus, the god of leadership and leader of the gods,
> and Athena, goddess of heroic endeavour and wide counsel,
> be with you on your continuing journey

NOTES

ABOUT THIS BOOK

1 Nanson, P. (2019) *Stand Up Straight: Ten Life Lessons from the Royal Military Academy, Sandhurst* (London: Penguin Random House).

1 BEGINNING LEADING GREAT LEADERS SELECT THEMSELVES – OR DO THEY?

1 Thody, A. (2003) 'Followership in educational organizations: a pilot mapping of the territory', *Leadership and Policy Journal*, 2(2): 141–156.
2 I made what I believe is an irrefutable case for interdisciplinary studies in schools (and in life!) in my 2015 book: Kerry, T. (2015) *Cross-curricular Teaching in the Primary School*, 2nd edition (London: Routledge). Chapters 1 and 2 describe the issues at length.
3 The DfE paper can be found at www.gov.uk/government/publications/teachers-standards.

3 THINKING IN A CRISIS PANIC DESTROYS REASONED THOUGHT

1 Wade, P. et al. (2007) *The Impact of School Fires* (London: NFER and LGA).
2 Definition by the American Psychological Association, www.apa.org/topics/resilience.
3 This article was: 'Record levels of stress put teachers at breaking point'. Appeared 10 November 2019

4 ONLY THE BEST – ADOPTING A QUALITY STANDARD THE SWAGGER STICK OF LEADERSHIP

1 The Department for Education (2009) *Improving Schools Programme Handbook*. It is typical of its genre (and now rather tired), but may be worth a look.

5 THE LEADER AS A TEAM PLAYER BONDING, VALUING, AND LISTENING TO THE BAND

1 The Teacher Education Project was designed to disseminate and publish good practice in training Secondary PGCE student teachers; it produced a wide range of publications and was very active over its four-year life and subsequently. The Schools' Council was a school-based research-orientated body, again predicated on teachers involving themselves with generating and disseminating good classroom practice; its publications were widely applauded by the profession but the government of the time (the funding body) did not feel it had enough control over teacher activity. The Funding Agency for Schools was concerned more with school organisation and management issues than with classroom teaching and explored many aspects of improved use of school time.

2 Belbin wrote many books which are easy to track down on the internet, e.g., *Management Teams: Why They Succeed or Fail* (1981) and *Team Roles at Work* (1993) are most relevant here.

3 You can find a visual of the spin wheel at www.trooping-the-colour.co.uk/trooping/trooping.htm.

6 SETTING AN EXAMPLE – HAVING A VISION AND LEADING FROM THE FRONT DEVELOPING THE COURAGE TO LEAD

1 Lt Col Tim Collins' speech appears at several internet sites and is worth reading in full: simply Google his name.

9 BECOMING ÉLITE: DEVELOPING AND FURTHERING YOUR SKILLS STAND STILL TO DROP DEAD: THE NEED TO ADVANCE YOUR LEADERSHIP SKILLS AND CAREER

1 The gurus of heutagogy were Stewart Hase (an Australian academic) and Chris Kenyon (a former wing commander in the RAAF). Their book is Hase, S. and Kenyon C. (2013) *Self-Determined Learning: Heutagogy in Action* (London: Bloomsbury). My chapter described applying the principles of heutagogy to an MSc course in education leadership.

2 The Chartered College of Teaching is a free-standing learned society based in London which evolved out of the former College of Preceptors and the former College of Teachers. Its activities can be viewed at www.charteredcollege. Bodies like the Chartered College and those in your curriculum fields are worthy of exploration as a means to professional development.

10 LEADERS IN CONTEXT LEADERSHIP ACROSS INSTITUTIONAL STYLES

1 www.verywellmind.com/what-is--laissez-faire-leadership-2795316#

2 Skogstad, A., Einarsens, S. and Torsheim, T. (2017) 'The destructiveness of laissez-faire leadership behaviour', *Journal of Occupational Health Psychology*, 12(1): 80–92.

3 Tony Bush's books are useful; see his *Theories of Educational Leadership and Management*, 4th edition (London: Sage). I find John West-Burnham's titles (various, on a range of topics, so Google him) more than averagely insightful.

INDEX

Academies 62, 63
Academy, Britehope 1
Adler, Alfred 56
ambiguity 106

Belbin, Meredith 51–52, 111
Bloom, Benjamin 6
business xii, 37–38

Collins, Tim Col. 66, 111
communication, effective 23, 77
conferences 91
confidence 27, 34, 107
courage 56–66, 100, 107
course leader 29, 75
critical incidents 32–33

Dawkins, Richard 62
Davies, Brent 87
Department for Education 6, 110

élites 89–98

failure 27, 30, 41
followers 2, 3, 5, 31
followers, types of 4
followership 1
Funding Agency for Schools 50
future, the 104

guesswork, intelligent 73

heads of department 10–13, 75–76
heutagogy 94, 111
hierarchies 80, 104

improving schools 36
independence 56
innovation 41
inspiration 1
issues, ethical 42

journals 91, 98
James, Clive 34

Kishimi, I. 56, 57

leaders xii, 5, 9, 29, 39, 57, 59,
    104, 107
leaders, middle 91, 95
leadership 14, 25, 36, 40, 61,
    66, 86, 90
leadership, bureaucratic 100–101
leadership, charismatic 99–100, 102
leadership, higher degrees in 89–98
leadership, laissez-faire 102–103, 112
leadership, styles of 99–105
leadership, transactional 103–105
leadership, transformational 103–105

leading 14, 56, 78–79
learning 82, 95
Lewis, C.S. 50
log, reflective 32–33, 80–81

management, of class 43, 78, 83
management, in education 14,
    19–25, 78, 93
management, teachers' tasks
    16–19, 45
manager, line 37, 84
managers, hotel industry 10–13
managing 14–25, 28
Meindl, James 50–51
mental health 81
mission 35, 107
Morris, Desmond 43
motivation 41, 95, 104

Nanson, Major General xi, 14, 26,
    32, 44, 98, 110
N.F.E.R 28, 110

Ofsted 28

planning 67–74, 85
positivity 38
professional development 89–98
professionalism 1, 6–7

quality 35, 37, 40, 42, 44

research 36, 89, 93, 95–98
research, in house 95–96
resilience 27, 29–30, 107
respect 45

school, curriculum 69–72
school, human resources of 69–72
school, plant 69–72
Schools' Council 50
scrutiny, external 42
self-belief 35
self-determination 56–57
self-discipline 14, 107
self-knowledge 32
skills 9–10, 26
SMEALCS 67–74, 107
spin wheel 55
stress 27, 30–31, 84, 107, 110
success 27, 30

Teacher Education Project 50, 111
team players 46, 49
team teaching 47–48
teams 45–55, 107
Teaching, Chartered College of
    98, 111
technology, educational 108
Thody, Angela 2–3, 7, 110
time, institutional 82–84
time, management of 88
time, organizational 84–86
time, personal use of 79–82
time, use of 23, 78–87, 107
timing 106, 108

vision 1, 35, 40, 67, 69–70, 107

warrant officer 10–13
Weber, Max 100
weaknesses, allowable 52
Wragg, E.C. 45

Printed in the United States
By Bookmasters